KU-506-541

Effective
Business Writing

THE LEARNING CENTRE
HAMMERSMITH AND WEST
LONDON COLLEGE
GLIDDON ROAD
LONDON W14 9BL

WITHDRAWN

HAMMERSMITH WEST LONDON COLLEGE

328542

THE SUNDAY TIMES

CREATING SUCCESS

Effective
Business Writing

Patrick Forsyth

KOGAN
PAGE

London and Philadelphia

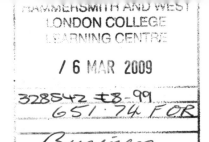

HAMMERSMITH AND WEST
LONDON COLLEGE
LEARNING CENTRE

/ 6 MAR 2009

328542 £8-99
651·74 FOR
Business

Publisher's note

Every possible effort has been made to ensure that the information contained in this book is accurate at the time of going to press, and the publishers and author cannot accept responsibility for any errors or omissions, however caused. No responsibility for loss or damage occasioned to any person acting, or refraining from action, as a result of the material in this publication can be accepted by the editor, the publisher or any of the authors.

First published in Great Britain and the United States in 2009 by Kogan Page Limited

Apart from any fair dealing for the purposes of research or private study, or criticism or review, as permitted under the Copyright, Designs and Patents Act 1988, this publication may only be reproduced, stored or transmitted, in any form or by any means, with the prior permission in writing of the publishers, or in the case of reprographic reproduction in accordance with the terms and licences issued by the CLA. Enquiries concerning reproduction outside these terms should be sent to the publishers at the undermentioned addresses:

120 Pentonville Road
London N1 9JN
United Kingdom
www.koganpage.com

525 South 4th Street, #241
Philadelphia PA 19147
USA

© Patrick Forsyth, 2009

The right of Patrick Forsyth to be identified as the author of this work has been asserted by him in accordance with the Copyright, Designs and Patents Act 1988.

ISBN 978 0 7494 5453 1

The views expressed in this book are those of the author, and are not necessarily the same as those of Times Newspapers Ltd.

British Library Cataloguing-in-Publication Data

A CIP record for this book is available from the British Library.

Library of Congress Cataloging-in-Publication Data

Forsyth, Patrick.
    Effective business writing / Patrick Forsyth.
        p. cm.
    ISBN 978-0-7494-5453-1
    1. Business writing. 2. Business communication.   I. Title
    HF5718.3F667 2008
    651.7'4--dc22
                            2008040876

Typeset by Saxon Graphics Ltd, Derby
Printed and bound in India by Replika Press Pvt Ltd

328542

For Frances Kay
This one has to be for you; thanks again for your help and
support (and wise words about e-mail).

(Frances Kay is an author with several successful business
books to her name, including *Brilliant Business Connections*.
She is also the editor of Kogan Page's excellent directory,
The Good Non Retirement Guide.)

Contents

Preface

In the interest of security please ensure that your door is fully closed firmly before entering or leaving your room.

Sign on the inside of hotel room doors – and a good trick if you can do it.

The sign quoted above makes a point: someone not only wrote this, they had it printed and posted on over 200 doors and apparently still didn't notice that it was nonsense. In the workplace, and elsewhere too, successful communication can often be difficult, and poor communication can cause problems. This may involve a momentary hiatus as two people try to sort out exactly what was meant. Or it may lead to a major misunderstanding that causes a project of some sort to be stopped in its tracks or a reputation to crumble. Why is this? There are many reasons, but one is certainly an assumption that what is being done is surely not difficult; for the most part we muddle through and hope to get there somehow in the end. If we don't, and if breakdowns in communication continue to occur, then some rethinking may prove useful.

Furthermore some kinds of communication are inherently more difficult than others. The intentions of communication may vary. It may need to inform, explain, motivate, challenge, prompt a debate or more; and such intentions are not mutually exclusive:

one communication may need to do several of these things at once. It may well prove difficult to succeed in even the simplest of these. Perhaps a message is simply superfluous, like the motorway sign saying 'This sign is not in use'. Sometimes the message may be muddled, but the true meaning can be inferred, as with the sign at the zoo that said 'Bring one child and another goes free' (What? Released into the wild?) Or the health and safety newsletter's item about bouncy castles under the heading 'Inflatable children's play equipment'. It might also be affected by moving from one language to another as was presumably the case with the notice in the bathroom of a hotel in Portugal that said 'Please ensure that mat is affixed firmly to bottom before entering shower.'

On other occasions messages may end up meaningless:

> To talk about information is to talk about objectives. A lot of thought is now being applied throughout the NHS to mission statements and objectives, from which we should obtain a clearer view of our information needs. However, objectives will never stand still, and therefore an information strategy will of necessity be a continuously developing concept. The process of clarification will be incremental, and the concept of a definitive strategy will remain illusory.

Yes, well, passing over the idea of objectives never standing still, this simply gets lost amidst its own pretensions. It is from a Regional Health Authority report quoted in the press.

Sometimes too it is the pretension that seems to produce the over-engineering. For example this description: 'a new and improved pest control system that utilises a percussive device with a planar surface and orthogonal contoured extension to instantly kill insects stone dead'. What? It means hitting the bug with a hammer when it is on a flat surface! So, any communicating clearly needs some care. Even when care is being taken additional complications may contrive to compound the issues.

There is a further problem, and that is that most people are better at communicating face-to-face than in other ways. Other methods all have their disadvantages. The telephone is good, immediate, maybe quick and easy, but try describing to someone over the telephone how to, say, tie a shoelace. Think about it for a second. You know how to do it, you could show someone – but, on the telephone, using only your voice, it is somehow more of a problem.

Maximum difficulty

One method that seems consistently to render people less articulate is when they have to put something in writing. Your manager wants a note about it, the board members need a report or proposal, my editor wants a book (and there are still nearly 40,000 words to go!). Business writing almost seems to hinder good communication. People who can talk about something and usually get their message over successfully, find themselves descending into a muddle and writing something over-formal, over-long and – at worst – forgetting somewhere along the way exactly what their objectives were in the first place. Technical matters and technology make things worse. This: 'We provide the leading business-to-business solution for clinical data capture and management for the pharmaceutical and biotech industry' probably means 'We streamline processes to speed important new drug therapies to market.'

If the style is archaic and the language is labyrinthine; if it is replete with sesquipedalians, places its full points over-long distances apart and allows an element of galimatias to act to confuse and obscure the sense – and another thing, it is without structure. Sorry, try again. If you write something full of long words and long sentences, which has no recognisable structure to guide you through, it is likely to fail. Incidentally, 'sesquipedalian' is a long word, takes one to know one I suppose, and 'galimatias' is gibberish. I know it says on the book's cover that there would be no – inappropriate – long words used in this book and here are two before we even reach Chapter 1; but they are only there to illustrate what to avoid. Just to get all this out of the way, 'hippopotomstros-esquipedaliophobia' is a fear of long words; perhaps something from which all business writers should aim to suffer.

Even one wrong decision can render a written document inef-fective. For example, consider this case: in a new job and charged with making radical changes, Mary found every plan she put forward to her boss was rejected. An examination of the tone of her proposals showed why. What she was writing was something like 'This system is not working well and could be corrected by...', albeit coupled with a perfectly sensible sugges-tion. But who had originated the system she planned to change? Her boss. In effect she was saying 'Your system's no good, I can suggest something better.' A change of tone to one that posi-tioned the suggestion carefully in time terms – 'This system has worked well in the past; in future we must find a way of also accommodating... so building in the following changes will...' – reversed the reaction. It really was only the implied criticism of past action that produced the negative reaction. A minor change to the way such proposals were written was enough to change their reception. Such seemingly minor matters are often instrumental in dictating outcomes.

Actually putting something into written form can be a chore, and its being so can extend the task, as agonising over the best form of words to make permanent takes time. Hence this book: the intention here is clear. It is to assist the process of communi-cating successfully when it must be done in writing. This may mean a letter or an e-mail, or it may mean a report, a proposal or various kinds of letter and document in between. It might also mean copy for a brochure or a newsletter. A message may be sent internally: to a group of staff or an individual member of a manager's team – or upwards, perhaps to your manager. It may be sent externally: to a supplier or a customer. The circumstances can vary. But the intention is always the same. It is to put across a message to someone else that will be understood, that will achieve its purpose and that will perhaps impress in the process.

Whatever your circumstances, this book has the aim of helping you see more clearly how to tackle business writing effectively. There is no one magic formula, as so often what makes a business technique work is, though it may be based on certain fundamental approaches, a matter of attention to a number of details. Certainly that is the case here.

It is, however, possible. You *can* write clearly and powerfully if you go about it in the right way, and if you do that, you will also begin to do it faster as well. In a busy life that is something worthwhile too. In the next few chapters we will see how all this can be done, starting with a look at some of the inherent problems.

Patrick Forsyth
Touchstone Training & Consultancy
28 Saltcote Maltings, Maldon, Essex CM9 4QP
patrick@touchstonetc.freeserve.co.uk

Introduction: problems and opportunities

I love being a writer. What I can't stand is the paperwork.

Peter De Vries

In a busy business life, writing anything can seem a chore. There are surely more important things to be done – people to meet, decisions to be made, action to be taken. Yet all of these things and more can be dependent on written communication. A letter or memo may set up a meeting, a report may present a case and prompt a decision, a proposal may act persuasively to make sure certain action is taken or a particular option is selected.

But reading business papers can be a chore also, and they will not achieve their purpose unless they are read, understood and do their job well enough to actively prompt the reader to action. The first rule is to accept that: Business writing must earn a reading.

The nature of written communication

You are probably both a reader and a writer of business documents. Consider the nature of the written word with your reader's hat on for a moment. Do you read everything that crosses your desk? Do you read every word of the things you do read? Do you read everything from the first word through in sequence, or do you dip into things? Almost certainly the answers make it clear that you do not treat all written material equally. Some documents are more likely to be read than others. Of course, some subjects demand your attention. Who ignores a personal note from the managing director? But the fact that some things have to be read often does not make their reading any easier or more pleasurable.

Good writing, which means, not least, something that is easy to read and understand, will always be likely to get more attention than sloppy writing. Yet we all know that prevailing standards in this area are by no means universally good.

Why is this? Maybe it is education; or lack of it. Often school (sometimes even university) assists little with the kind of writing we find ourselves having to do once we work in an organisation. Maybe it is lack of feedback; perhaps managers are too tolerant of what is put in front of them. If more poor writing were rejected and had to be rewritten, then more attention might be brought to bear on the task.

Habits are important here too. We all develop a style of writing and may find it difficult to shift away from it. Worse, bad habits may be reinforced by practice. For example, word-processing means that the ubiquitous standard document can often be used year after year with no one prepared to say 'Scrap it', even if they notice how inadequate it is.

First principles

It is easy to make fun of slips of the pen (or mind?) The government's Environment Agency recently announced that it had 'helped to make our environment a safer place by managing a UK scheme to dispose of surplus radioactive sources in schools, museums and hospitals'. Are your kids glowing in the dark? Or is this somewhat badly worded? We can learn more from the approach taken to writing than from the one odd phrase. So at this stage, let's analyse writing through an example, and review a typical business letter. Many of us have probably received something like this, usually addressed by name and slipped under the door to greet us as we rise on the last day of a stay in a hotel. The example that follows is a real one, though the originator's name (a Singapore hotel) has been removed.

Dear Guest,

We would like to thank you for allowing us to serve you here at the XXXX Hotel and hope that you are enjoying your stay.

Our records show that you are scheduled to depart today, and we wish to point out that our check-out time is 12 noon. Should you be departing on a later flight, please contact our front desk associates who will be happy to assist you with a late check-out. Also, please let us know if you require transport to the airport so that we can reserve one of our luxury Mercedes limousines.

In order to facilitate your check-out for today, we would like to take this opportunity to present you with a copy of your updated charges, so that you may review them at your convenience. Should you find any irregularities or have any questions regarding the attached charges, please do not hesitate to contact us.

We wish you a pleasant onward journey today, and hope to have the privilege of welcoming you back to the hotel again in the near future.

Sincerely yours,

(Name)
Front Office Manager

Note: Before reading on, and bearing in mind what has been said so far, you might like to consider this example in some detail. Ask yourself what its purpose is and how well it achieves it. Check whether you understand it, and see if you find its tone – addressing a guest of a hospitality business – suitable. Make notes of any comments you have, which you can refer back to later.

Now let me offer some observations – what are we to make of such a letter? It is, necessarily, a standard one used many times each day. It came to my notice when it arrived under my door and, taking note of the bit about late checkouts, ' will be happy to assist you', I went to Reception to take advantage. Not only was I told 'Sorry, we're too full to do that today', so were a dozen other people during the 10 minutes I stood at the desk. So, the first thing to say is that the letter is so badly expressed that it does more harm than good, causing as much disappointment as satisfaction because it says clearly that something *will happen* when it should really say something may only *sometimes* be possible.

It is also very old fashioned with rather pompous sounding phrases such as: 'we wish to point out that' and 'we would like to take this opportunity', when something shorter, more straightforward and businesslike would surely be better. It almost *suggests* that the account may be wrong ('irregularities'), and everything is expressed from an introspective point of view: 'We', 'we' and 'we' again leading into every point. No, it is not good and your own analysis may well run longer.

The key problem is perhaps intention. What is the letter designed to do?

- Simply to remind people to pay the bill?
- To make checkout quicker or easier?
- To sell a transport service to the airport?
- To persuade people to come and stay again (and thus presumably give an impression of efficiency and good service)?
- Just to say 'Thank you'?

Because it mixes up all of these to some extent, it fails to do justice to any of them. For example, nothing about the checkout procedure is explained, nor are reasons given as to why someone should stay again. Yet this is surely a straightforward letter; perhaps that is why it was given inadequate thought. As well as making an immediate point about standard letters – use them by all means, but make sure they are good – it leads neatly to the next point.

A fragile process

We can all recognise the really bad report, without structure or style, but with an excess of jargon and convoluted sentences and which prompts only one thought: 'What is this trying to say?' But such documents do not have to be a complete mess to fail in their purpose. They are inherently fragile. One wrongly chosen word may dilute understanding or act to remove what would otherwise be a positive impression. Even something as simple as a spelling mistake (and, no, computer spellchequers – sic – are not infallible) may have a negative effect.

I will never forget, in my first year in a consulting firm, playing a small part in proposals that were submitted to a dairy products company. After meetings, deliberations and more meetings, a written proposal was sent. A week passed. Then an envelope arrived from the company concerned. Inside was a single sheet of paper. It was a copy of the title page of the proposal and on it was written, in red ink the three words 'No thank you'; this alongside a red ring drawn around one typed word. The word 'Dairy' in the company's name had been spelt 'Diary'. For a long while after that everything was checked very much more carefully. The moral is clear.

As a very first rule to drum into your subconscious – check, check and check again. Mistakes that remind us to do so are on public display (like the rather surreal one I saw recently in a lift that said 'Only use the buttons provided').

Whether the cause of a document being less good than it should be is major or minor, the damage is the same. The quality of writing matters.

A major opportunity

Whatever the reasons for poor writing may be, suffice it to say that if prevailing standards are low, then there is a major opportunity here for those who better that standard. More so for those who excel; and, remember the permanence of the written word – your bad documents might just come back to haunt you later.

So, effective business writing is a vital skill. There may be a great deal hanging on a document doing the job it is intended to do – accurate action, a decision, a sale, a financial result, or a personal reputation. For those who can acquire sound skills in this area very real opportunities exist. The more you write, and the more important the documents you create, the truer this is. Quite simply, if you write well then you are more likely to achieve your business goals.

This point cannot be overemphasised. One sheet of paper may not change the world, but – well written – it can influence many events in a way that affects results and those doing the writing. And you can write well. We may not all aspire to or succeed in writing the great novel (mine is still on Chapter 1), but most people can learn to turn out good business writing – writing that is well tailored to its purpose and likely to create the effect it intends.

Good business writing need not be difficult. It is a skill certainly, but one that can be developed with study and practice. Some effort may be involved, and certainly practice helps, but it could be worse. Somerset Maugham is quoted as saying: 'There are three rules for writing the novel. Unfortunately, no one knows what they are.' Business writing is not so dependent on creativity, though this is involved, and it is subject to certain rules. Rules, of course, are made to be broken, but they do act as useful guidelines and can therefore be a help. Here, in reviewing how to go about the writing task, I will mention something about when to follow the rules and when to break them. So, what makes good business writing?

The hazards of communication

Despite predictions about the 'paperless office', offices seem as surrounded (submerged?) by paper as ever. Indeed as documentation is essentially only a form of communication, this is likely to remain so. However a message is put over, even if there is no paper, as with something sent through e-mail for example, it has to be written.

With no communication any organisation is stifled; indeed nothing much would happen. Communication – good communication – should oil the wheels of organisational activity and facilitate action. This is true of even the simplest memo, and is certainly so of something longer and more complex like a report.

Communication is – inherently – inclined to be less than straightforward. If this is true of tiny communications, how much more potential for misunderstanding does a 25-page report present? And with written communication the danger is that any confusion lasts. There is not necessarily an immediate opportunity for the reader to check (the writer might be a hundred miles away), and a misunderstanding on page 3 may skew the whole message and negate the purpose of an entire report.

Serious, and very serious

Once something is in writing any error that causes misunder-standing is made permanent, at least for a while. The dangers of ill-thought-out writing are varied. It may:

■ *be wrong*, but still manage to convey its meaning, like the cookbook that advises: 'To stop your eyes watering when chopping onions, put them in the freezer'. Or the Air New Zealand advertisement that offered: 'Round the world tickets from £698 return'. I love the thought of a round the world trip that somehow fails to return. Such things may amuse, but will probably be understood. No great harm done perhaps, though the first might just throw doubt on the credibility of the recipe. Indeed, any fault tends to high-light the possibility of other, more serious, problems;

■ *try too hard to please*, ending up giving the wrong impres-sion. In one Renaissance Hotel there are signs on the coffee shop tables that say: 'COURTESY OF CHOICE: The concept and symbol of "Courtesy of Choice" reflect the centuries-old philosophy that acknowledges differences while allowing them to exist together in harmony. "Courtesy of Choice" accommodates the preferences of individuals by offering both smoking and non-smoking areas in the spirit of conviviality and mutual respect.' An absurd over-politeness just ends up making the message sound rude – this restaurant has both smoking and non-smoking areas and if you find yourself next to a smoker – tough. It does matter;

■ *be incomprehensible*. A press release is an important piece of writing. One, quoted in the national press recently, was sent out by the consulting group Accenture. The item commented that Accenture envisioned: 'A world where economic activity is ubiquitous, unbounded by the tradi-tional definitions of commerce and universal'. Er, yes – or rather, no. The newspaper referred not to the content of the release, only to the fact that it contained a statement so wholly gobbledegook as to have no meaning at all. It is sad when any writing is so bad that it achieves less than nothing;

■ *Be nonsense.* A cooker advertisement says 'Neff's Circosteam doesn't have complicated functions – just simple one-touch controls, including 52 cooking programmes' (and that's simple?). And be careful if all this gives you a headache: one pack of pills suggests that you 'swallow with a glass full of water'. A glassful is less likely to stick in your throat.

You could doubtless extend such a list of examples. The point here is clear: it is all too easy for the written word to fail. All the above were probably the subject of some thought and checking; but not enough. Put pen to paper and you step onto dangerous ground.

So, the first requirement of good business writing is clarity. Think of how regularly you are faced with brief e-mail messages and, because they are ambiguous in some way, simply have to reply asking for clarification. Much time is wasted this way. Similarly, a good report needs thinking about if it is to be clear, and it should never be taken for granted that understanding will be automatically generated by what we write.

It is more likely that we will give due consideration to clarity, and give the attention it needs to achieving it, if we are clear about the purpose of any document we may write.

Why are you writing?

Exactly why anything is written is important. This may seem self-evident, yet many reports, for instance, are no more than something 'about' their topic. Their purpose, if they have one, is not clear. Without clear intentions the tendency is for the report to ramble, to go round and round and not come to any clear conclusion.

Documents may be written for many reasons. For example they may be intended to inform, motivate or persuade and often more than one intention is aimed at, and different messages or emphasis for different people can add further complexity.

Reader expectations

If a document is to be well received, then it must meet certain expectations of its readers. Before going into these let us consider generally what conditions such expectations. Psychologists talk about what they call 'cognitive cost'. This is best explained by example. Imagine you want to programme the video recorder. You want to do something that is other than routine, so you get out the instruction book. Big mistake. You open it (try this, you can open it at random) and the two-page spread shouts at you 'This is going to be difficult!' Such a document has what is called a 'high cognitive cost' (that is, the cost in time and aggravation of understanding something), rather than appearing inviting. Even a cursory look is off-putting.

People are wary of this effect. They may even look at a document almost *expecting* reading it to be hard work. If they discover it looks easier and more inviting than they thought (a low cognitive cost), then they are likely to read it with more enthusiasm. What gives people the feeling, both at first glance and as they get further into it, that a document is not to be avoided on principle?

In no particular order, the following are some of the key factors of reader preference. They like it – and are more likely to give something their attention – if a document is:

■ *brief:* obviously something shorter is likely to appear to be easier to read than something long, but what really matters is that any document is of an appropriate length for its topic and purpose. Perhaps the best word to apply is *succinct* – to the point. A report may be 10 pages long, or 50, and still qualify for this description;

■ *succinct:* this makes clear that length is inextricably linked to message. If there is a rule, then it is to make something long enough to carry the message – then stop;

■ *relevant:* this goes with the first two. Not too long, covering what is required, and without irrelevant content or digression. Note: comprehensiveness is *never* an objective. If a report, say, touched on everything possible, then it would certainly be too long. In fact, you *always* have to be selective, and if you do not say everything, then everything you do say poses a choice – so, you need to make good content choices (as I know all too well, such choice consumes a considerable amount of the time spent writing a book like this one);

■ *clear:* readers must be able to understand it. This applies in number of ways; for example, it should be clearly written (in the sense of not being convoluted), and use appropriate language – you should not feel that, as an intended reader, you have to look up every second word in a dictionary.

■ *precise:* saying exactly what is necessary and not constantly digressing without purpose;

■ *in 'our language':* in other words using a level and style of language that is likely to make sense to the average (or intended) reader, and which displays evidence of being designed to do so;

■ *simple:* avoiding unnecessary complexity (more of this anon);

■ *well structured:* so that it proceeds logically through a sequence that is clear and appears to be a sensible way of dealing with the message. It may be useful to both describe the structure used and explain why it is appropriate to readers;

■ *descriptive:* again, we return to this later; here it suffices to say that if there is a need to paint a picture it must do so in a way that gets that picture over.

All these have in common is the fact that they can act to make reading easier. Further, they act cumulatively; that is, the more things are right in each of these ways, the clearer the writing will be. If the impression is given that effort has *actively* been made to making the reader's task easier, then this is so much the better.

Both the above factors are worth personalising to the kind of people to whom you must write. Whether this is internal, a colleague perhaps, or external, you need to be clear what your communications have to do and what kinds of expectations exist for them at the other end. For example, a technical person may have different expectations from a layperson, and may be looking to check a level of detail that must exist and be clearly expressed for a document to be acceptable to him or her. Always focus on your recipients in this way as you write.

The readers' perspective

It follows logically from what has been said in this chapter so far that good business writing must reflect the needs of the reader. Such writing cannot be undertaken in a vacuum. It is not simply an opportunity for the writer to say things as he or she wants. Ultimately only readers can judge a document to be good. Thus their perspective is the starting point and as the writer you need to think about whom the intended readers are, how they think, how they view the topic that you are writing about, what their experience to date is of the issues, and how they are likely to react to what you have to say.

Powerful habits

Habit, and the ongoing pressure of business, can combine to push people into writing on 'automatic pilot'. Sometimes, if you critique a piece that you wrote, or that went out from your department, you can clearly see something that is wrong. A sentence does not make sense, a point fails to get across, or a description confuses rather than clarifies. Usually the reason this has occurred is not that the writer really thought this was the best sentence or phrase to use, and got it wrong. Rather it was because there was inadequate thought of any sort, or none at all.

Habits can be difficult to break and the end result can be a plethora of material moving around organisations couched in a kind of gobbledegook or what some call 'office-speak'.

Earning a reading

The moral here is clear. Good writing does not just happen. It needs some thought and some effort (and some study, with which this book aims to assist). The process needs to be actively worked at if the result is going to do the job you have in mind, and do it with some certainty. But good habits are as powerful as are bad. A shift from one to another is possible and the rewards in this case make the game very much worth the candle. Think what good writing skills can achieve.

The rewards of excellence

Consider the example of reports; they can influence action. But they also act to create an image of the writer. Within an organisation of any size, people interact through communication. They send each other e-mails, they sit in meetings and on committees, they chat as they pass on the stairs, or share a sandwich at lunchtime; and everything about the way they do all this sends out signals. It tells the world, or at least the organisation, something about them. Are they knowledgeable, competent, expert, decisive and easy to deal with – would you take their advice, follow their lead or support their cause?

All the different ways in which people interrelate act together, cumulatively and progressively, to build up and maintain an image of each individual. Some ways may play a disproportionate part, and report writing is one such. There are two reasons why this effect is important. First, all documents, unlike more transient means of communication, can last. They are passed around, considered, and may well remain on the record; more so if they are about important issues. Secondly, because not everyone can write effectively, people can be impressed by a clear ability to marshal an argument and put it over in writing.

Thus business writing represents an opportunity, or rather two opportunities. Business writing – at least when it is good – can be instrumental in prompting action; action you want, perhaps. It is also important to your profile. What you write says something about the kind of person you are, how effective you are and what you are like to work with. In a sense there are situations where you want to make sure certain personal qualities shine through. A case may be supported by it being clear that someone who gives attention to details, for instance, is presenting it.

Longer term the view taken of someone by their superiors may be influenced by their regularly reading what they regard as good reports. So, next time you are burning the midnight oil to get some seemingly tedious report finalised, think of it as the business equivalent of an open goal and remember that it could literally be affecting your chances of promotion!

A significant opportunity

Many business documents demand detailed work. Their preparation may, on occasion, seem tedious. They certainly need adequate time set aside for them. But as the old saying has it: if a job is worth doing, it is worth doing well. It may take no more time to write effectively than it does to do so in a lacklustre way; this is so for a report, e-mail or for any other document. Indeed, the next chapter contends that a systematic approach can speed up your writing.

If whatever you write is clear, focused and set out so as to earn a reading, then you are more likely to achieve your purpose. In this case too, good writing is also more likely to act positively to enhance the profile of the writer. Both these results are surely worthwhile. But the job still has to be done, the words still have to be got down on paper, and faced with a blank sheet of paper (or, these days, computer screen) this can be a daunting task (and surely writing a book of this length qualifies me to say that!). Go about it in the right way, however, and it does become possible.

Before we turn to the process of writing, let us summarise certain key points made so far:

- Remember communication has inherent dangers; clear communication needs to be well considered.
- Messages will only achieve their purpose if the writer is clear in their mind what they are seeking to achieve.
- The reader is more important than the writer; write for others not for yourself.

- Beware old habits (that serve you ill) and work to establish good ones.
- What you write is potentially a powerful tool – powerful in action terms, and powerful in contributing to your personal profile.

2

Getting the right words down

> All the words I use... can be found in a dictionary – it's just a matter of arranging them into the right sentences.
>
> *Somerset Maugham*

In this chapter, which unashamedly parallels a chapter from another book in this series, *How to Write Reports and Proposals,* we look at how you get set to write something in a way that will be likely to make it effective, and specifically at how you start the actual process of writing. Knowing you have to write something (especially a long something) can prompt different responses in different people: you may put it off, doodle, or write some central part quickly and ahead of the rest 'because you know that'. Whatever you do now, whatever your current habits are, you might want to consider the exercise below before continuing with this chapter.

Exercise

It might be useful, at this point, to have something that you have written by you as you read on, and to think particularly about *how* it got written. In other words, what procedure and actions, in what order, went into drafting it.

You can do this in three ways:

1. Wait until you have a drafting job to do, do it, keep a note of how you went about it and have it by you as you read on.
2. Write something (or at least start to) as an exercise and use it as a guideline to your current style and practice.
3. Locate something (preferably recent, so that you still have the details of it in mind) from the files, and make some notes as to how you composed it to refer to while reading on.

Think before writing

Few areas of business skill can be acquired through some magic formula, and business writing is no exception. However, preparation perhaps comes close to acting in this way. It really is the foundation upon which successful writing is based. Preparation allows you do two things. First, it will help create a document that not only you feel content with, but one that has a clear purpose and which is regarded as useful by its readers. As has been said, the ultimate measure of good business writing is whether it achieves the outcome you wish.

Secondly, a systematic approach to preparation and writing will save you time. This is a worthy result in its own right. Which of us does not have too much to do? When I first had to do a significant volume of writing, and thus looked into what made it work well in order to improve my own practice, the way I worked did change. It was a matter of some surprise to me that whatever effect this may have had on what I wrote, I found I was getting my writing done more quickly. This experience has been found also by many people I have met through conducting training on this topic and is, I am sure, something you may find too.

In this chapter, therefore, we review the actual process of preparation and getting the words down. First things first. We will start with what you should not do. Do not, faced with the task of writing, say, what looks like being a 20-page report, get out a clean sheet of paper and immediately start writing the first words: '1. Introduction. This report sets out...'. Thinking must precede writing. In other words you need to engage the brain before your hands. Yet many people start all their writing this way: they start writing and planning together.

Why are you writing?

Like so much in business, any business document – even a short e-mail – needs clear objectives. Let us be specific about that. Objectives are not what you wish to *say*, they are what you wish to *achieve*. Put simply, the task is not to write, say, 'about the new policy'. Rather it is to ensure people understand the proposed change and how it is intended to work. This in turn is designed to ensure people accept the necessity for it and are prompted to undertake their future work in a way that fits with the new policy.

Once this is clear in your mind the writing is already likely to be easier. With a more specific situation (perhaps the topic you took for the exercise above), objectives can be formed precisely if, as the much-quoted acronym has it, they are SMART. That is:

Specific
Measurable
Achievable
Realistic
Timed

As an example of this principle, imagine you are setting up a training course on the subject of report writing. What objectives would you set? Using the SMART principle, the course should:

■ enable participants to ensure future reports are written in a way that will be seen by their readers as appropriate, informative and, above all, readable (*specific*);

■ ensure (*measurable*) action occurs after the session – eg future proposals might be measured by the number of recipients who subsequently confirmed agreement;

■ be appropriate for the chosen group – eg an inexperienced group might need a longer and more detailed programme than a group consisting of people with more experience – and thus have *achievable* objectives;

■ be not just achievable but *realistic* – eg the time away from the job might be compared with the potential results springing from the course to ensure attendance was desirable; and

■ be *timed*: when is the workshop? In a month or in six months? And how long will it last? One day? Two days? Results cannot come until it has taken place.

In addition, any objectives should be phrased more in terms of readers than of the writer, and overall the following two key questions must be answered clearly: *Why* am I writing this? *What* am I trying to achieve?

To check if an answer to either is too vague to be useful, say of it 'Which means that...' and see if this leads to a more specific statement. For example, you might say simply that such a course is designed to improve writing skills. So far so good, but what does this mean? It means that documents will be less time-consuming to prepare than in the past, more reader-oriented and more likely to achieve their objectives. This line of thinking can be pursued until objectives are absolutely clear.

Once your objectives are set satisfactorily you can proceed to the real business of getting something down on paper, though this still does not mean starting at the beginning and writing on to the end.

A systematic approach

It is a rare person who can write at any length without making a few notes first, and frankly the complexity of many documents often demands a little more than this. Sometimes all that is necessary is a dozen words on the back of the proverbial envelope, but you need to be very sure that you are not missing anything. Unless you are thoroughly prepared, the chances are that whatever you create as your first draft will be somewhat off target, and time must then be spent tinkering and reworking it to get it into order. Typically this is more than would have been taken giving it more thought in the first place.

Another danger is time. Writing may fail only because it is rushed (and therefore thinking is insufficient). Or time problems are compounded by deadlines. And who never has to work to tighter deadlines than they would like? Too often skimping preparation, combined with a pressing deadline, means that something must be submitted even though the writer knows that an additional review and some more editing would make it more likely to do its job well.

So, to encompass all possibilities and degrees of complexity, the following staged approach sets out a method that will cope with any kind of document, short or long (it is the way this book began life too). It is recommended only by its practicality. It works. It will make the job quicker and more certain. It can install the right habits and rapidly become something you can work with, utilising its methods more or less comprehensively, depending on the circumstances.

Each of the stages is reviewed in turn. As was said earlier, you may want to follow this with an example in mind. If you want an example, just for this exercise, that you can pitch into quickly and easily, imagine that you have to write something about your job. To make it more interesting, and give it a specific objective, imagine that what needs to be written is a letter designed to attract internal candidates to apply for your job because (we can imagine what we like) you are to be promoted – only once a successful applicant is found.

The following provides a pathway. You can follow it or adapt it. You can shortcut it somewhat, especially for straightforward documents, but not too much – omitting significant elements of the different stages can make writing slower and more awkward, and allow the end result to be less good than would otherwise be the case.

Stage 1: Research

This may or may not be necessary. It may be that everything you need is already in your head. On the other hand it may be that you need to do some digging, or at the least some assembling. For example, let us suppose you are writing about one of your company's products. It may make sense to get together previous documents describing it, technical literature, even the product itself, and have these to hand as you commence the job. It may be that you need to cast the net wider; in this case what about competitive product material, for example? Similarly, to create continuity, if writing something like a newsletter, you would sensibly have any earlier issues to hand.

There is no hard and fast rule here. You should, however, ask yourself what might be useful and take a moment to collect and look at or read what the task suggests is necessary.

Stage 2: List the content

Next, ignoring just for the moment sequence, structure and arrangement, just list – in short note (or keyword) form – every significant point you might want to make. Give yourself plenty of space; certainly use one sheet of paper as it lets you see everything at a glance without turning over. Put the points down, as they occur to you, at random across the page.

You will find that this process (which is akin to mind-mapping) acts as a good thought-prompter. It enables you to fill out the picture as one thing leads to another, with the freestyle approach removing the need to think or worry about anything else or even how to link points together. The scale of this stage may vary.

Sometimes it is six words on the back of an envelope, more often somewhat more on an A4 sheet (and this book started life on a sheet of flipchart paper divided into squares for the chapters).

Stage 3: Sorting it out

Now you can bring some sort of order to bear. Review what you have noted down and decide on:

- the sequence in which points should go;
- what logically links together;
- what is ancillary, providing illustration, evidence or example to exemplify points made;
- whether the list is complete (you may think of things to add), or whether some things on it can be omitted *without* weakening the overall message. This latter point links to careful consideration of length; clearly most documents need to be contained to a degree.

The quickest and easiest way to undertake this stage is to annotate your original note, highlighting and amending it in a second colour. This is for your reference only; if you find it helpful to use arrows, circle words or draw symbols or pictures – fine, do so.

Stage 4: Arrange the content

Sometimes, at the end of the previous stage, you have a note you can follow and no more needs to be done. Often, however, what you have in front of you can be a bit of a mess. By arranging it I mean simply turning it into a neat list; this could also be the stage at which you type it out to finish the job on screen. Most people seem to input their own written material nowadays. (I sometimes think the typing is harder work that the writing!)

Final revision is, of course, still possible at this stage, but, that done (and it might include getting another opinion about it from, say, a colleague), you are left with a clear list setting out content, sequence and emphasis to whatever level of detail you find helpful. Some experimentation may be useful here; certainly I am not suggesting over-engineering the process. This sheet then becomes your blueprint from which you write. You must decide the form in which this is most useful.

Stage 5: A final review

This may not always be necessary, or possible (deadlines may be looming), but it can be useful to leave it a while – sleep on it – and only start writing after you come back to it fresh. You can get very close to things, and it helps you to see clearly if you step back and distract your mind with something else.

Now, with a final version of what is effectively your writing plan in front of you, you can – at last – actually draft the text.

Stage 6: Writing

Now you write; or type or dictate. This is where the real work is, though it is very much easier with a clear plan for the task. What you have done here is obvious, but significant. You have separated the two tasks: one of deciding *what* to write, the other of deciding *how* to put it. Being a bear of very little brain, I for one certainly find this easier; so too do many other people. Here are some further tips.

Choose the right moment: if possible pick a time when you are 'in the mood'. There seem to be times when words flow more easily than others. Also interruptions can disrupt the flow and make writing take much longer as you recap in your mind, get back into something and continue. It is not always possible, of course, but a bit of organisation to get as close as possible to the ideal is very worthwhile.

Keep writing: do not stop and agonise over small details. If you cannot think of the right word, a suitable heading – whatever – put in a row of Xs and continue. You can always return and fill in such gaps later, but if you lose the whole thread then writing becomes more difficult and will take longer to do.

Again, the idea of preserving the flow in this way can quickly become a habit, especially once you are convinced it helps.

So now you have a draft, though already you may feel that it needs further work. Now what?

Stage 7: Editing

Few – if any – people write perfect text first time and alter nothing. If you write, then some editing goes with the territory. So, rule one is not to feel inadequate, but to accept that this is the way it works and allow a little time for revision. Careful preparation, as suggested in earlier stages, should minimise alterations; at least you should not be finding things you have left out or altering the whole structure. The words may need work, however. Computer spelling and grammar checkers are very useful. Be warned: not every spelling inaccuracy is corrected (for example, *their* and *there*); proper names and such-like may need care too. Grammar checkers should not be followed slavishly, especially for the punchy style you need for some business messages. Perhaps a sensible rule here is not to ignore anything highlighted as grammatically incorrect *unless* you can give yourself a good reason for so doing.

Editing may be helped by:

■ *sleeping on it* (as mentioned earlier);
■ *getting a colleague to check it* (maybe you can do a swap with someone else who would value your looking at some of their written material – it is amazing how a fresh eye and brain pick up things to which you are, or have become, blind. Incidentally, listen to what they say and consider it carefully: it is easy to become defensive and reject what, with hindsight, may turn out to be good advice);
■ *being thorough* (do not regard editing as a chore; it is an inherent part of getting something right).

Editing is an important stage. Seemingly small changes: replacing a word, breaking a long sentence into two, adding more and better placed punctuation – all may make a real difference. This is the time to bear in mind style and use of language (see the next chapter) as well as sense and clarity. Then when you are happy with it let it go, press *print* or whatever comes next. It is easy to tinker for ever. You will always think of something else that could be put differently (better?) if you leave it and look again, but productivity and deadlines are important too.

Let your version of this systematic approach become a habit and you will find your writing improves, and that actually writing gets easier. As a rule of thumb, allow a proportion of the total time you allocate, or simply need for writing, for preparation. If you find that, say, 15–30 per cent of the time, or whatever works for you, is necessary, you will also find that rather than 'additional' preparation increasing the overall task time, such jobs actually begin to take less time. Simply pitching in and starting immediately at the top of a blank sheet of paper (or computer screen) with no preparation is just *not* the quicker option that perhaps it sometimes seems to be.

If you are conscious of how you write and think about what makes the writing process easier or more difficult for you, then you will no doubt add to this list and adopt further ways that help you. Of course, at the same time we must be realistic. There are things that interfere with how you would like to write, including deadlines that prohibit putting it off and other priorities˙and interruptions. The right attitude here involves two things.

First, do not let perfection be the enemy of the good; in other words, get as close as you can to your ideal way of operating. Do not let problems make you see the whole thing as impossible and abandon your good intentions entirely. Secondly, use habit to build up greater writing strength, for instance persevering with something until you *make it work for you*. For example, I used to be rather poor at writing on the move, but a busy life and regular travel made it necessary. Nowadays, after some perseverance, I can tune out the hustle and bustle of, say, a busy airport and get a good deal done.

A systematic approach really is half the battle. Try it, and remember to:

- go about the task of writing systemically;
- create and work to a writing plan;
- separate deciding *what* you are going to include (content) from *how* you are going to put it (style), thus giving yourself two separate tasks rather than one more complex one;
- fix on an approach that suits you and stick with it, creating useful, individual habits in the process;
- give the task space and priority;
- Check, check and cheque (sic) again.

Note: you may want to have a look at an example you may have been using before moving on to the next chapter.

3

Using language effectively

> 'When I use a word,' Humpty Dumpty said in a rather scornful tone, 'it means what I choose it to mean – neither more nor less.'
>
> *Lewis Carroll*

English is a powerful language. Its vast vocabulary allows precise description. Its oddball rules, however, can make for difficulty. Consider the following (in part adapted from an internet posting):

Why is it that: Writers write, but hammers don't ham?

Quicksand works slowly, boxing rings are square and a guinea pig is neither from Guinea nor a pig?

The plural of goose is geese, but we don't say one mouse and two meese?

We can make amends, but not when things are not so serious, just make one amend?

If you have odds and ends in a drawer and clear everything up, you don't know whether the last thing you take out is an odd or an end?

And why is abbreviated such a long word?

In English people recite at a play and play at a recital, we ship things by truck and send cargo by ship; we have noses that run and feet that smell. A fat chance and a slim chance mean the same thing, but a wise man and a wise guy are opposites. Your house can burn down as it burns up, you fill in a form by filling it out and an alarm goes off by going on.

And all this while ignoring the added complexity of technical matters – for example, who decided that we should switch off a computer by clicking on 'Start'? And was English their first language?

No wonder writing can be difficult. Words do matter, and so too do many other things about language. The precision with which you use it can make or break even a simple written message. Before tackling anything more complicated let's consider words; simple single words, no problem there surely? Well, perhaps there is.

The difference a word makes

Saying something is 'quite nice' is so bland that, if applied to something that is *hugely enjoyable* it understates it so much as to be found almost insulting. The emphasis may be inadequate but at least the word 'nice' makes it clear that something positive is being said; more on the danger of blandness later.

Blandness is certainly one thing to be avoided, and is unlikely to add power to your message, but choosing the wrong word is another matter. Doing so might well confuse, upset – or worse. The following examples are designed to show the danger. Let us start with a couple of simple everyday words: 'comic' and 'comical'. Mean much the same thing? No. Something 'comic' is intended to be funny, whereas something 'comical' is funny unintentionally. That's put banana skins in their place, but more relevant to business writing are the following:

■ *Continuous* (unbroken or uninterrupted); *continual* (repeated or recurring) – a project might be continuous (in process all the time), but work on it is more likely to be continual (unless you never sleep).

■ Are you *uninterested* in a proposal or *disinterested* in it? The first implies you are apathetic and care not either way, the latter means you have nothing to gain from it.

■ Similarly *dissatisfied* and *unsatisfied* should not be confused. They mean disappointed or needing more of something, respectively.

■ You might want to do something *expeditious* (quick and efficient), but saying it is *expedient* might not be so well regarded as it means only that something is convenient (not always a good reason to do anything).

■ *Fortuitous* implies something happening accidentally; it does not mean fortunate.

■ If you are a *practical* person then you are effective, if something is *practicable* it is merely possible to do, and *pragmatic* is something meant to be effective (rather than proven to be so).

So, even one wrong word may do damage. More can quickly create nonsense: 'This practicable approach will ensure the practicable project will be continuous; it is fortuitous that I am uninterested in it and I am sure I will not be unsatisfied to see it start.' Some words are regularly misused: objectives and strategies, turnover and profit, and more. Care is called for literally word by word.

Of course no inaccurate use of language will help you get over your message even if it only annoys rather than confuses: as, for example, saying 'very unique' might do – 'unique' means unlike anything else and cannot be qualified in this way – a particular twitch of mine, this one. Some care, maybe even some checking or study, may be useful, so let's consider some other areas of language use.

Sex... and other unmentionables

These days it is incumbent upon us all to be politically correct. I probably shouldn't use the word 'sex' as a heading, though it is fun to have an excuse to do so and it is well known that books mentioning sex sell better than those that don't. More seriously, sexist language, together with inappropriate references to age, religion, ethnic origin and so on, is not just unsuitable, but can get you into serious trouble. Even minor transgressions can get people thinking of you in the wrong way.

I am sure I have no need to dwell on obvious examples; even an idiot would not write in a way that insults his or her readers; and that phrase is (intentionally) sailing close to the wind to make a point. What needs to be done is to keep an eye on the way language is used and the way you use it. Changes need to be made from the past, but always clarity must shine through – it is no good being politically careful but misunderstood. For example:

■ *The he/she conundrum:* these days most people avoid an exclusive use of 'he' in case that seems to imply men only. Yet using 'she' throughout seems pretentiously contrived, and writing 'he or she' repeatedly quickly becomes awkward and tedious, so a mixture of avoidance techniques is perhaps best. Gradually the use of 'their' is changing so that writing that, 'the boss called us into their office' is now usually grammatically acceptable.

■ *Time and terminology:* some words go through an evolution of usage. 'Chairman' is the sort of word that these trends largely outlawed, at least for a while; but now, although there is much use of 'Chair', many women seem happy to be 'Chairman'. This sort of thing needs an eye keeping on it.

■ *Silly:* sometimes suggested changes seem to go too far. For example, I was pulled up the other day for talking about 'manning the office'. You should say, 'staffing' someone told me. But surely 'staffing the office' means recruiting people to work there, and 'manning it' means deciding who is on duty at different times to provide coverage. Change here seems to me to risk a lack of clarity (and wouldn't doing so be just a little over-sensitive?)

This is an area that changes as you watch and there is certainly some silliness and over-sensitivity in evidence, but it is important and deserves some careful consideration. Some mistakes are very much to be avoided, and you must write to fit particular and current practice.

Other mistakes to avoid

A number of things may act to dilute the power of your writing. They may or may not be technically wrong, but they end up reducing your effectiveness and making your objectives less certain to be achieved. Here are some examples.

Blandness

Watch out! As has been said, this is a regular trap for the business writer, but it is worth emphasising here. A bland feeling occurs not so much because you *choose* the wrong thing to write, but because you are writing on automatic pilot *without* thought, or at least much thought, for the detail and make no real conscious choice.

What does it mean to say something is:

- *quite* good (or bad);
- *rather* expensive;
- *very* slow progress?

What exactly is:

- an *attractive* promotion (as opposed to a profit-generating one, perhaps);
- a *slight* delay (for a moment or a month?);
- *some* improvement;
- a *practical* approach?

All these give only a vague impression. Ask yourself exactly what you want to express, and then choose language that does just that. For example, is a 'practical approach' one that is easy to do, quick to do – or both or something else altogether?

I had a sobering reminder of this recently when I wrote something for a publisher with guidelines forbidding the use of the word 'key'. What I was writing was aimed at readers in the business world where this is a word that tends to crop up regularly: key issues, key objectives and more.

The instruction made me think. I checked another recent manuscript, clicking on Find and listing the key (sic) word. I was amazed how many times it appeared in a manuscript of, I think, 40,000 words. Alongside this I began to think of alternatives. I looked up the word 'crucial' in my Thesaurus and went on from there. Soon I had listed many alternatives – pivotal, critical, central, significant, and more – many of which, with precise and slightly different meanings, substituted for 'key' in a way that was more appropriate, and made the writing stronger and better. I duly avoided the word 'key' in the piece of writing in question and resolved to double-check its appropriateness every time I was tempted to use it elsewhere in future. You too may have favourite words you over-use and which could be replaced by words that are more accurately descriptive.

'Office-speak'

This is another all too common component of some business writing, much of it passed on from one person to another without comment or change. It may confuse little, but adds little either, other than an old-fashioned feel. It includes phrases such as:

■ 'Enclosed *for your perusal*' (or 'enclosed *for your interest*') may be unsuitable. You may need to tell them why it should be of interest; or 'enclosed' alone may suffice).

■ *We respectfully acknowledge receipt of* (why not say: 'Thank you for…'?)

- ■ *In the event that* ('if' is surely better).
- ■ *Very high speed operation* (fast, or state just how fast).
- ■ *Conceptualised* (thought).

Avoid such trite approaches like the plague (sic – see comment on clichés in due course), and work to change the habit of any 'pet' phrases you use all too easily, all too often – and inappropriately. Avoid also sounding as if your main reference is not a dictionary but a jargon generator. Phrases like 'strategic', 're-engineered paradigm', 'proactive', or 'virtual integrated opportunity' just prompt the reaction 'What?' – or 'Idiot'.

Language of 'fashion'

Language is changing all the time. New words and phrases enter the language almost daily, often from the United States and also linked to the use of technology. It is worth watching for the lifecycle of such words because if you are out of step then they may fail to do the job you want. I notice three stages:

1. When it is too early to use them. When they will either not be understood, or seem silly or even like a failed attempt at trendiness.
2. When they work well.
3. When their use begins to date and sound wrong or inadequate.

Examples may date too, but let me try. When BBC Radio 4 talks about an 'upcoming event', then for some people this is in its early stage and does not sound right at all; 'forthcoming' will suit me well for a while longer.

On the other hand, what did we say before we said 'mission statement'? This is certainly a term in current use. Most people in business appreciate its meaning and some have made good use of the thinking that goes into producing one.

What about a word or phrase that is past its best? To suggest a common one: 'user-friendly'. When first used it was new, nicely descriptive and quickly began to be useful. Now with no single gadget on the entire planet not so described by its makers, it has become weak to say the least.

Mistakes people hate

Some errors are actually well known to most people, yet they still slip through. There is a category that shares the characteristic that many people find them annoying when they are on the receiving end. A simple, but important example, mentioned earlier, is the word 'unique', which is so often used with an adjective. 'Unique' means something is like nothing else. Nothing can be 'very unique' or 'greatly unique'; even the company whose brochure I saw with the words 'very unique' occurring three times in one paragraph does not in fact have a product that is more than just 'unique', even once. Think of similar examples that annoy you and avoid them too.

Others here include the likes of:

- *different to* (different from);
- *less* (which relates to quantity, when number – where fewer would be correct – is involved);
- *can* being confused with *may* (possible and permissible respectively).

Another area for care is with unnecessary apostrophe's (sic), which is becoming a modern plague (here even Lynne Truss's wonderful book *Eats, Shoots and Leaves* has not reversed the trend).

Clichés

This is a somewhat difficult one. Any overused phrase can become categorised as a cliché. Yet a phrase like 'putting the cart before the horse' is not only well known, but establishes an instant and precise vision – and can therefore be useful. In a sense people like to conjure up a familiar image and so such phrases should not always be avoided, and business documents may not be the place for creative alternatives like 'spreading the jam before the butter'.

Following the rules

What about grammar, syntax and punctuation? Of course they matter, so does spelling, but spellcheckers largely make up for any inadequacies in that area these days; though you need to cheque (sic) carefully – there are plenty of possibilities for error. But some of the rules are made to be broken and some of the old rules are no longer regarded as rules, certainly not for business writing.

Certain things can jar. Consider just a couple of examples:

■ *Poor punctuation:* too little is exhausting to read, especially coupled with long sentences. Too much becomes affected seeming and awkward. Certain rules do matter here, but the simplest guide is probably breathing. We learn to punctuate speech long before we write anything, so in writing all that is really necessary is a conscious inclusion of the pauses. The length of pause and the nature of what is being said indicate the likely solution. In some ways better too much than not enough.

■ *Tautology* (unnecessary repetition) of which the classic example is people who say 'I, myself personally', which is to be avoided. Do not 'export overseas', simply export, do not indulge in 'forward planning', simply plan.

■ *Oxymoron* (word combinations that are contradictory) may sound silly or inappropriate – 'distinctly foggy', 'fun run' – or be current good ways of expressing something – 'deafening silence'. Some sentences can cause similar problems of contradiction – 'I never make predictions; and I never will.'

Other things are still regarded as rules by purists, but work well in business writing and are now in current use. A good example here is the rule stating that you should never begin a sentence with the words 'and' or 'but'. But you can. And it helps produce tighter writing and avoids overlong sentences. But... or rather however, it also makes another point: do not overuse this sort of thing.

Another similar rule is that sentences cannot be ended with prepositions. Yet 'He is a person worth talking to' really does sound easier on the ear than: '...with whom it is worth talking'. Winston Churchill is said to have responded to criticism about this with the famous line: 'This is a type of arrant pedantry up with which I will not put.'.

Still other rules may be broken only occasionally. Many of us have been brought up never to split infinitives, and it thus comes under the annoyance category most of the time. There are exceptions however: would the most famous one in the world – Star Trek's, 'to boldly go where no man has gone before' – really be better as, 'to go boldly...'? I do not think so.

Making language work for you

How language is used makes a difference to exactly how a message is received. The importance of using the right word has already been touched on, but the kind of difference we are talking about can be well demonstrated by changing no more than one word. For example, consider the first sentence after the last heading: 'How language is used makes a difference to exactly how a message is received.' Add one word: '...makes a *big* difference to...'.

Now let us see what changing that word 'big' makes: it is surely a little different to: '...makes a *great* difference...'. There are many alternatives, all with varying meaning: real, powerful, considerable, vast, special, large, important – you can doubtless think of more. In the context of what I am actually saying here, 'powerful' is a good word. It is not just a question of how you use language, but what you achieve by your use of it.

Note: no business writer should be without both a dictionary and a Thesaurus beside their desk; and the latter is often the most useful.

Making language descriptive

Let's not dwell on mistakes, but think positive. The language is on your side. It is perfectly possible to create powerful descriptions; often this can be done in remarkably few words. The following description (from Peter Mayle's book *A Year in Provence*) describes a visitor to the house. He arrives with an attractive young lady (who is described in some detail) and he shows her up the steps ahead of him. The only thing that is said about him is that he was 'A man who could give lessons in leering.' Is there anything else you need to know? Even something as routine as a classified advertisement can make the point. For example: 'For sale: baby's cot – unused'. Have you ever read an ad that conjures up so much heartache?

Often business writing is almost wholly without adjectives. Yet surely one of the first purposes of language is to be *descriptive*. Most writing necessitates the need to paint a picture to some degree at least. Contrast two phrases: 'smooth as silk' and 'sort of shiny'. The first (used as a slogan by Thai Airways) conjures up a clear and precise picture; or certainly does for anyone who has seen and touched silk. The second might mean almost anything: dead wet fish are sort of shiny, but they are hardly to be compared with the touch of silk. Further, an even more descriptive phrase may be required. What about something I heard on the radio: 'slippery as a freshly buttered ice-rink'. Could anyone think this meant anything other than *really, really* slippery?

The question of expectation of complexity (and cognitive cost) was mentioned earlier, and to some extent it does not matter whether something is short or long, whatever it is – if it makes things effortlessly clear, it is appreciated. And if it is both descriptive and makes something easier to understand then readers are doubly appreciative.

Clear description may need working at, but the effort is worthwhile. Trainers often ask meeting venue staff to set up for a seminar arranging a group 'in a U-shape'. You can put people in a U around a boardroom-style table. But more often trainers mean a U in the sense of an open U, one that gives the trainer the ability to stand within the U to work and communicate with delegates. There are, in fact, two different layouts here, which both demand precise description.

Description is important, but sometimes we want more than that. We want an element of something being descriptive, and also *memorable*. This is achieved in two ways: first by something that is descriptive yet unusual; secondly, when it is descriptive and unexpected.

Returning to the venue theme above, if a conference executive describes, as part of an explanation about room layouts, a U-shape as being one that 'puts everyone in the front row' they are being descriptive and memorable because, while clear, it is also an unusual way of expressing it (and just how a trainer sees it). Such phrases work well and are thus worth searching for.

As an example of the second route to being memorable, I will use a description I once put in a report. In summarising a Perception Survey (researching the views customers and contacts held of a client organisation) I wanted to describe how the majority of people reported. They liked the organisation, were well disposed towards using it, but also found it a little bureaucratic, slow and less efficient and innovative than they would ideally like. I wrote that the organisation was seen as 'being like a comfortable, but threadbare old sofa, when people wanted them to be like a modern, leather executive chair'. This is clearly descriptive, but it gained from being not just unusual, but really not the kind of phrase that is typically used in business writing. Its being memorable was confirmed, because it rang bells and at subsequent meetings was used by the organisation's own people to describe the changes that the report had highlighted as necessary.

There are occasions when this kind of approach works well, not least in ensuring that something about the writer is expressed along the way. Some phrases or passages may draw strength because the reader would never feel it was quite appropriate to put it like that themselves, yet find they like reading it.

Another aspect you may want, on occasion, to put into your writing is emotion. If you want to seem enthusiastic, interested, surprised – whatever – this must show. A dead, passive style: 'the results were not quite as expected; they showed that…' is not the same as one that characterises what is said with emotion: 'you will be surprised by the results, which showed that…'. Both may be appropriate on occasion, but the latter is sometimes avoided when it could add to the sense and feeling; and there might be occasion to strengthen that – 'the results will amaze'.

Consider this. How often when you are searching for the right phrase do you reject something as either not sufficiently formal or conventional? Be honest. Many are on the brink of putting down something that will be memorable or that will add power, and then they play safe and opt for something else. The alternative selected may be adequate, but may fail to impress; and may well then represent a lost opportunity. It works best to write closer to how you would *say* things. Certainly thinking of what you would say and then formalising it (a bit) is better than disappearing into some vision of 'how formal business writing should be'.

Next, we look at some things to avoid.

Personal style

Most people have, or develop, a way of writing that includes things they simply like. Why not indeed? For example, although the rule books now say they are simply alternatives, some people, myself included, think that to say: 'First, …', 'secondly…', 'and thirdly…', has much more elegance than beginning: 'Firstly…'. The reason why matters less than achieving an effect you feel is right.

It would be a dull old world if we all did everything the same way, and writing is no exception. There is no harm in using some things for no better reason than that you like them. It is likely to add variety to your writing, and make it seem distinctively different from that of other people, which may itself be useful.

Certainly you should always be happy that what you write *sounds* right. So, to quote the writer Keith Waterhouse: 'If, after all this advice, a sentence still reads awkwardly, then what you have there is an awkward sentence. Demolish it and start again.'

4

Making it persuasive

You don't have to compromise your integrity to sell.
You simply have to find and emphasise the things
that unite you, instead of the things that divide you.

John J Johnson

Now, recognising the difficulties of making communication
work, we go beyond them and look at what creates a message
that acts to persuade, and see how your writing can relate to the
way in which people make decisions to act.

People are often suspicious of someone 'with something to sell'.
Persuasion is synonymous with selling and selling does not have a
very good image. Consider your own reaction to someone trying
to sell you double glazing or insurance, particularly when it is done
inexpertly or inappropriately; every persuasive message prompts a
little of the reaction generated by the worst kind of selling.

The process in view

Your approach must reduce and get over this kind of feeling.
How do you do this? Essentially you start by adopting the right

attitude to the process. Before you write anything you are going to need to approach it in the right way. Persuasion must *not* be regarded as a process of 'doing something to people'; rather it should be seen as working *with* people. After all any communication inherently involves more than one person. People presented with a possible course of action will want to make up their own minds about it; indeed, they will instinctively weigh up the case presented to them and make a considered decision.

The amount of conscious weighing up undertaken will depend on how people judge the import of the decision to be made. Ask someone in the office 'Will you spare some time for a drink at lunchtime so that we can discuss the next scheduled departmental meeting?' and they may hardly need to think about it at all. It is only a few minutes, they have to have a bite to eat anyway, and they already know about the meeting and want to be involved. Ask, or write to them, about something more substantial and the weighing up process will involve more, maybe much more.

If you want to define persuasion it is perhaps best described as being a process of helping people weigh something up and make a decision about it; literally, when you aim to persuade you are *helping people decide*. It follows therefore that you need to understand how they actually go about this process. In simple terms, paraphrasing psychologists who have studied it, this thinking process can be described thus; people:

- consider the factors that make up a case;
- seek to categorise these as advantages or disadvantages;
- weigh up the complete case, allowing for all the pluses and minuses;
- select a course of action (which may be simply agreeing or not, or involve the choice of one action being taken rather than another) that reflects the overall picture.

Let us be clear. What is going on here is not a search for perfection. Most things we look at have some downsides; this may be the most useful book you ever read, but reading it does take a little time, and that could be used for something else. This time disappearing might well be seen as a downside. The weighing scales analogy is worth keeping in mind. It can act as a practical tool, helping you envisage what is going on during what is intended to be a persuasive conversation. Beyond that it helps structure the process if you also have a clear idea of the sequence of thinking involved in this weighing up process.

The thinking process

One way of looking at what is going on is to think of people moving through several stages of thinking, as it were saying to themselves:

■ *I matter most.* Whatever you want me to do, I expect you to worry about how I feel about it, respect me and consider my needs.

■ *What are the merits and implications of the case you make?* Tell me what you suggest and why it makes sense (the pluses) and whether it has any snags (the minuses) so that I can weigh it up, bearing in mind that few, if any, propositions are perfect.

■ *How will it work?* Here people also want to assess the details not so much about the proposition itself but about the areas associated with it. For example, you might be wanting to persuade someone to take on, or become involved with, a project. The idea of the project might appeal, but, say, it ends with them having to prepare a lengthy written report they might see that as a chore and therefore as a minus and might, if the case is finely balanced, reject it because of that.

■ *What do I do?* In other words, what action – exactly – is now necessary? This too forms part of the balance. If something seen in a quick flick through this book persuaded you that it might help you, you may have bought it. In doing so you recognised (and accepted) that you would have to read it and that this would take a little time. The action – reading – is inherent in the proposition and, if you were not prepared to take it on, this might have changed your decision.

It is after this thinking is complete that people will feel they have sufficient evidence on which to make a decision. They have the balance in mind, and they can compare it with that of any other options (and remember, some choices are close run with one option only just coming out ahead of others). Then they can decide; and feel they have made a sensible decision, and done so on a considered basis.

This thinking process is largely universal. It may happen very quickly and might be almost instantaneous – the snap judgement. Or it may take longer, and that may sometimes mean days or weeks (or longer!) rather than minutes or hours. But it is always in evidence. Because of this, there is always merit in setting out your case in a way than sits comfortably with the way in which it will be considered. Hence the definition describes persuasion as *helping the decision-making process*.

This thinking process should not be difficult to identify with; it is only what you do too when you consider buying something or have a decision to consider. Essentially all that is necessary when attempting to persuade is to keep it in mind and address the individual points in turn. Thus you need to:

▨ *Start by demonstrating a focus on the other person* – it helps also to aim to create some rapport and make clear how you aim to put things over (making clear, for example, how you plan to go through something).

▨ *Present a balanced case* – you need to stress the positive, of course, but not to pretend there are no snags, especially if manifestly there are some; so present a clear case, give it sufficient explanation and weight and recognise the balancing up that the recipient will undertake.

▨ *Add in working details* – mention how things will work and include ancillary details, especially those that will matter to others.

When you set out a case the structure and logic of it should sensibly follow this pattern. Otherwise the danger is that you will be trying to do one thing while the person you are communicating with is doing something else. They will do what they want, and especially so when they are reading something – and you are not there to try to draw them back to your logic.

Persuasion's magic formula

The dictionary says of the word 'persuasion': to cause (a person) to believe or do something by reasoning with them. Fine, but the question is *how* to do this. To be persuasive a case must be *understandable, attractive* and *credible*. Let's consider these in turn.

Creating understanding

A good deal has been said in other chapters about the need for clear communication. The point here is more than simply avoiding misunderstandings. People like clarity of explanation and ease of understanding. Making readers spend five minutes reading endless pages that go round the houses about something, only to have light dawn at the last moment in a way that gets the person thinking 'Why ever didn't you say that to begin with?' hardly builds your credibility.

When people find something easy that they expect to be difficult to understand, they like it. A powerful description, especially one that puts things in terms the other person can identify with, can strengthen a case disproportionately. Care is sensible here. Avoid inappropriate use of jargon: it is only useful shorthand when both parties have the same level of understanding of the terminology involved. You only have to think about computers to observe the problem. So, always:

■ think about explanations and descriptions, try them out and be sure they work;

■ aim to make what you write immediately and easily understood;

■ be thorough and precise, giving people enough detail to make the point and emphasising the most relevant elements;

■ match the level of technicality you use with the other person (and avoid or explain jargon if it might confuse).

This is an area where you can score some points. Think about the structure and sequence of what you write and how it breaks down into subsections, present a logical and organised case and signal what you aim to do in advance; 'It may be easiest if I present this in stages. Let me refer to the timing first, then the costs, and then how we need to organise implementation.' If such a start gets people nodding ('That seems sensible') then you will carry them with you to the next pages. Use as many layers of this as is necessary to keep things clear. For example, in the above example add 'timing implies when we will do things and how long it will take, so duration is taken first; then it is easier to see when things can be fitted in'.

Already what you achieve in this respect can begin to put some convincing pluses on the positive side of your balance.

Making the case attractive

This part of the argument has to set out the core pluses of the case, painting a picture of why agreement should follow. You get your own way when people see what something does for, or means to, them. How this is done is largely a question of giving the argument a focus on what, in sales jargon, are called 'benefits' rather than 'features'. So, a *benefit* is what something does for or means to someone, while *features* are simply factual points about it.

The spellchecker on a computer is a feature. Being able to produce an accurate manuscript quickly and easily, the time and effort saved and the avoidance of material being returned for correction (by a boss, customer or, for an author, an editor) are all benefits. They are things the feature – the spellchecker – brings me. Features act to produce benefits.

The sequence here is important. Just tell people everything about a suggestion in terms of its features and their response may well be to say (or think) 'So what?' Start by focusing on what they want (you may need to discover this), show them that what you are suggesting provides it, and then the feature may reinforce the argument.

Benefits in action

You could say something will 'save you money' (saving something you want to save is always a benefit, as is gaining anything positive), or that it will 'save money and recoup its cost in a month', or 'it will halve what you spend'. If the description matches the circumstances of the reader and if it specifically rings bells because of how it is described, then this will work best. Consider a product example. A company sells commercial cooking equipment to restaurants and cafes. One product is flat grills. One feature is the size: there are various models and one has a cooking surface of 800 square centimetres. What is the benefit? 'It will cook a dozen eggs or six steaks simultaneously.' Now most people find it difficult to conjure up 800 square centimetres in their mind's eye, but *everyone* who runs a restaurant will be able to imagine the eggs and steaks with no problem at all. Link the way this is described to their situation further – 'imagine the rush you get at breakfast time' – and it makes a powerful point.

If you always keep in mind what something does for or means to other people, you will be able to write text that will put over a more powerful case. The phrase 'benefit-led' is used in selling and that is a good way of thinking about it. Benefits come first, features explain how that is possible and, if necessary, you can add additional credibility (of which more anon). For example:

> This book is called *Effective Business Writing* (feature). It will help you get a message across effectively and, when necessary, to obtain agreement from others (benefit),

which will save arguments and get more done (further benefit). The methods it describes are tried and tested and their presentation in training courses has received positive feedback (evidence; to which might be added a positive comment from a named delegate or training organisation).

The idea of teasing out the way you put things by saying *which means that...* and seeing where that takes you is a good one; start with a feature and at the end of the line you will assuredly have a benefit – maybe more than one.

You can do worse than list all the things that people might obtain from your ideas prior to writing. Some may be classic (see the box below), others may be more individual to whatever you are writing about.

What's in it for me?

As a result of agreeing with you people might be able to:

- make more money;
- save money;
- save time, effort or hassle;
- be more secure;
- sort out problems;
- be able to exploit opportunities;
- motivate others (eg staff);
- impress people (eg customers).

As a further example, let's return to the earlier example of two people involved in a presentation. Say 'A rehearsal will only take an hour' (the duration is a feature) and it may leave someone cold or get them asking 'How long?' in horror at what they see as a long time. Get them agreeing that the presentation must go well – 'Yes, it must'; that there is a great deal to gain from it – 'Right'; and that there is a possibility of two presenters falling over each other's feet unless there is a rehearsal – 'Could be.' Then the 'ability of the rehearsal to increase the chances of success' (which is what it will do and is therefore a benefit) makes much better sense.

The task is therefore to make a clear case to people, to emphasise aspects of the case that reflect their priorities, and have a positive effect on the other person, and to make sure there are sufficient, and sufficiently powerful, pluses to add up to an agreeable proposition. But, as was said, there is a further element to making a persuasive case. It needs to be *credible*.

Adding credibility

Because of the inherent suspicion that tends to exist when selling or persuasion are in evidence, peoples' reaction to your saying that something is a good course of action to adopt may simply be to say 'You would say that wouldn't you!' Your say so is not enough. Never just rely on that alone, but seek and build in evidence. This could be sheer numbers ('thousands of customers can't be wrong'), or tests, guarantees or standards met or complied with. It must be clear that the case really is sound. The salesperson selling a car who says 'The Automobile Association test results show it does 55 miles per gallon' is putting a reliable source ahead of the figure they want to quote, and boosting the weight it adds to their argument. This makes it so much more likely to be believed than simply saying 'It will do 55 miles to the gallon.'

Such credibility can be added in many ways, for example:

■ Quoting past experience: 'the project approach is very like... and that worked well'.
■ Involving the support of others (a person or organisation): 'the Training Manager says a rehearsal of the presentation would be useful' (when the other party respects the person referred to).
■ Quoting measurement of results: '50 per cent of this kind of presentation end without securing agreement; let's make this one of the successful ones'.
■ Mentioning any guarantees, tests or standards that are met.

■ Invoking quantity that reinforces the case: 'Several departments work this way already/hundreds of people use it'.

It is worth thinking both about the need for proof and how strong that need might be, and thus what evidence can be used in support of your argument before exposing any case to others.

A final point here: remember that a person's perspective on something may not be solely their own. Someone might react with their employer or department, their boss, their family, or their staff in mind. Equally, they may react positively for reasons of common good, because their helping you will help make the department you both work for more efficient perhaps, or very personally – they want to be seen to be involved in something or you promise them a drink in the pub.

Using language persuasively

People seldom read a letter immediately, and rarely in the same sequence in which it was written. Their eyes flick from the sender's address to the ending, then to the greeting and perhaps the first sentence. They fix on headings, they skim to the end – and then, if the sender is lucky, back to the first sentence for a more careful reading of the whole letter from the beginning. A letter is just an example: the same principle applies to other documents, even a short e-mail.

You must always present a message people will really consider, and nowhere is this more true than when you aim to persuade. This is something worth bearing in mind as you write and reinforces the point made earlier about *earning a reading*. In fact for some writing it may be worth calling a powerful image to mind. I always think of the training film 'The Proposal' (Video Arts), which I sometimes use on courses. It starts with the sales person writing a proposal and imagining its receipt. We see the buyer (actor John Cleese) expressing overpowering delight at its arrival. He clears his desk, cancels meetings, tells his secretary he must not be disturbed and settles down to read. Then the voice-over says 'But it's not like that, is it?' The scene changes, and this time when the document arrives we see a surly John Cleese sitting miserably at his desk dropping Alka Seltzers into a glass and wincing at the noise they make. Maybe *that* is who we should imagine writing for!

A persuasive structure

Face-to-face you can adapt your approach to the individual you are with as the conversation proceeds. In writing this is not possible and a formula to structure the approach is useful. The classic sales acronym AIDA stands for:

Attention: first get them reading and wanting to know more.
Interest: then develop their interest and make them want to read on to complete the picture.
Desire: aim to turn just interest into an actual acceptance or wanting for something.
Action: conclude by asking clearly for the action you want to be taken.

This provides a simple structure and works well in providing a plan to help compose persuasive messages and represents accurately the job to be done in prompting a response. Each stage is worth a further word (with something the length of the classic letter primarily in mind as an example).

Attention – the opening
The most important part of any letter is the start. It may well determine whether the rest of the letter is read. The opening may be quite short – a heading (there should surely always be a heading), a couple of sentences, two paragraphs – but it is disproportionately important. A good start will help as you write the letter, as well as making it more likely the recipient will read it. Omit or keep references short and make subject headings to the point – the reader's point. Do not use 'Re' (meaning this is about...). It is old fashioned and was once used

in front of a heading to show that it was a heading before it was easy to do so with, say, bold type. Make sure the start of the letter will command attention, gain interest and lead easily into the main text. For example:

- ask a 'yes' question;
- explain why you are writing to that reader particularly;
- explain why the reader should read the letter;
- flatter the reader (carefully);
- explain what might be lost if the reader ignores the message;
- give the reader some 'mind-bending' news (if you have any).

Interest/desire – the body of the letter

The body of the letter runs straight on from the opening. It must consider the readers' needs or problems from their point of view. It must interest them. It must get them nodding in agreement: 'Yes, I wish you could help me on that.'

Of course (you say) you are able to help them. In drafting you must write what you intend for the readers and then describe the benefits you can offer (not features), and in particular the benefits that will help them solve their problems or satisfy their needs.

You have to anticipate the reader's possible objectives to your proposition in order to select your strongest benefits and most convincing answers. If there is a need to counter objections, then you may need to make your letter longer and give proof; for example, comment from a third party that the benefits are genuine. However, remember to keep letters as short as possible, though still as long as necessary to complete the case. If that takes two, three or more pages, so be it.

It is easy to find yourself quoting full chapter and verse down to the last detail. If you were writing a lecture on the subject, you would probably need all that information. More usually you have to select just the key benefits that will be of particular value to the reader and which support any accompanying literature.

The central text must:

- keep the reader's immediate interest;
- develop that interest with the best benefit;
- win the reader over with a second benefit and then further benefits to produce a powerful case.

The next job is to ensure action from the reader by a firm close. This may need to summarise, but beyond that the most important thing to do is to state, clearly, the action or agreement you want.

Securing agreement and prompting action

Next consider the final words used in persuasive writing and their relationship to your intention to prompt action. In 'closing' (as sales jargon calls it) it may be useful to make a (short) summary of the benefits of the proposition. Having decided on the action you want the reader to take, you must make it *absolutely clear to them what it is*. I was once involved in a project with a professional association that was changing its subscription arrangement so that payment had to be made by direct debit. The instructions seemed crystal clear, but people managed to misinterpret them somehow and the association's secretary's telephone rang regularly with members on the line with queries. If people can misinterpret something, they will, and you must... Enough. Suffice to say that any reference to action must be clear, and that means spelling it out *very carefully*.

Reply cards sent with (good) direct mail provide a lesson for us. They are as well produced and important looking as the rest of the shot. They often reinforce or repeat their message more than once. For example, the telephone number to be called is printed in bold, repeated and may well be highlighted in, say, colour. Similarly the instructions, carefully analysed, smack of belt and braces; it is perfectly sensible and worth learning from.

It is necessary to nudge the reader into action with a *decisive* close. Do *not* use phrases like these:

- 'We look forward to hearing...'.
- 'I trust you have given...'.

- '...favour of your instructions'.
- '...doing business with you'.
- 'I hope I can be of further assistance'.

Offer further assistance or information by all means, but don't suggest incompleteness or inadequacy, with phrases such as 'If you have any queries...'. Many such phrases are only really added as padding between the last point and 'Yours sincerely'. They are clichéd and add nothing except an old fashioned feel or, worse, a feeling of uncertainty and circumspection. Instead, use real closing phrases, such as the following.

The alternative close
- Ask the reader to telephone or write.
- Ask the reader to telephone or use the reply-paid envelope.
- Ask the reader to request a meeting or more information.

Immediate gain
A phrase like: 'Return the card today and your profitability could be improved' offers something extra, or seemingly extra, if action is taken now rather than later. The converse of this is called a *fear close,* for example phrasing something to say 'Unless you respond now' something good will be missed.

'Best' solution
This is a phrase that summarises key issues mentioned earlier: 'You want a system that can cope with occasional off-peak demands, that is easy to operate by semi-skilled staff and is presented in a form that will encourage line managers to use it. The best fit with all these requirements is our system X. Return the card indicating the best time to install it' that then links to a closing statement.

Direct request
Just a straight request, or even, on occasion, an instruction: 'Post the card back today. Telephone me without delay.'

An impersonal message can put people off taking action, so if it is something like a letter going to a list of people, make sure it is signed off appropriately. Writing to customers, consider too the person who should have their name at the bottom of the letter. Replies will tend to come back to them – and so will queries. So, for example, for a sales letter, should it be the sales office, one director or another, and how well are they able to cope with any response? Make sure the signatory's name is typed as well, as signatures tend to be awkward to read, and that a note of the position they hold in the firm is included. People like to know with whom they are dealing; indeed, they resent it if they do not.

PS

Remember the power of the postscript. Past practice will tell you they are for things inadvertently left out, but direct mailers (and research about it) will tell you they really do get read. Make sure their wording makes clear they are not about something accidentally omitted, but are there to provide emphasis. Use them to reinforce an important point or to add a final benefit – it can add strength to many messages.

An appropriate tone

Returning to the language you use: it must be clear, appropriate and have sufficient impact to persuade. The following points add to those made in the previous chapter, starting with a list that recaps and sets out some basic rules for persuasive copy:

- *Be clear.* Make sure that the message is straightforward and uncluttered by 'padding'. Use short words and phrases. Avoid jargon.
- *Be natural.* Do not project yourself differently just because it is in writing.
- *Be positive.* In tone and emphasis (be helpful).
- *Be courteous.* Always (ditto politically correct).
- *Be efficient.* Project the right image.

▪ *Be personal.* Use 'I' – say what *you* will do, though focus on the reader throughout.
▪ *Be appreciative.* 'Thank you' is a good phrase.

The next list examines certain specific aspects of the language usefully used in persuasive (and sales) communications. All these examples are very much the kind of language that does not lend itself to persuasion. While one or two such words or phrases may do no great harm, if this kind of style predominates then the tone set is wholly wrong. So:

▪ *Avoid trite openings*
  - We respectfully suggest...
  - We have pleasure in attaching...
  - Referring to the attached...
  - This letter is for the purposes of requesting...
▪ *Avoid pomposity*
  - We beg to advise...
  - The position with regard to...
  - It will be appreciated that...
  - It is suggested that the reasons...
  - The undersigned/the writer...
  - May we take this opportunity of...
  - Allow me to say in this instance...
  - Having regard to the fact that...
  - We should point out that...
  - Answering in the affirmative/negative...
  - We are not in a position to...
  - The opportunity is taken to mention...
  - Dispatched under separate cover...
▪ *Avoid coldness and bad psychology*
  - I would advise/inform...
  - Desire
  - Learn/note
  - Obtain
  - Regret
  - Trust

■ *Avoid clichéd endings*
  - Thanking you in advance...
  - Assuring you of our best attention at all times, we remain...
  - Trusting we may be favoured with...
  - Awaiting a favourable reply...
  - Please do not hesitate to...

Rather than this sort of thing, your text must be positive. It should say: 'This is the case; this will be what is done' and will rarely say things like 'I think', 'probably', 'maybe' or 'perhaps'.

Experienced direct mailers talk about 'magic' words, or at least words that inject a tone that should always be present; these can be consciously used in many different documents. Some examples appear below (and you may well be able to think of more).

Magic words

free	today	timely	introducing
guarantee	win	respected	
new	easy	reliable	
announcing	save	opportunity	
you	at once	low cost	
now	unique	fresh	

You must not overuse such words or your message will become blatantly over the top, but do not neglect them either.

You must keep searching for ways of making your chosen words perform better. Again, the following is designed not only to suggest and highlight some examples, but also to show the approach that you need to cultivate. The guidelines that follow are reviewed in terms of 'dos' and 'don'ts', with no apology for any occasional repetition.

The don'ts

You should *not:*

▥ *Be too clever:* it is the argument that should win the reader round, not your flowery phrases, elegant quotations or clever approach.

▥ *Be too complicated:* the point about simplicity has been made. It applies equally to the overall argument.

▥ *Be pompous:* this means saying too much about you, your organisation and your product/services/ideas (instead of what it means to the reader). It means writing in a way that is too far removed from the way you would speak. It means not following exact grammar too slavishly at the expense of an easy, flowing style (though take care).

▥ *Over-claim:* while you should certainly have the courage of your convictions, too many superlatives can become self-defeating. Make one claim that seems doubtful and the whole argument suffers. It ends up diluting your argument, annoying, reducing credibility and... enough, point made.

▥ *Offer opinions:* or at least not too many compared with the statement of facts, ideally substantiated facts.

▥ *Lead into points with negatives:* for example, do not say 'If this is not the case we will...'; rather 'You will find... or... '.

▥ *Assume your reader lacks knowledge:* rather than saying, for example, 'You probably do not know that...', it's better to say, 'Many people have not yet heard...', or: 'Like others, you probably know...'.

▥ *Overdo humour:* never use humour unless you are very sure of it. An inward groan as they read does rather destroy the nodding agreement you are trying to build. I noticed a huge poster atop a high building as I drove to Bangkok airport recently, which said that BMW was the 'torque of the town'. So clever, so funny – so yuk. A quotation or quip, particularly if it is relevant, is safer, and even if the humour is not appreciated, the appropriateness may be noted. I hope, incidentally, that this book makes you smile occasionally, but also that this intention is not overdone.

■ *Use up benefits early:* a persuasive case must not run out of steam. It must end on a high note and still be talking in terms of benefits even towards and at the end.

The dos

You *should* do the following:

■ *Concentrate on facts:* the case you put over must be credible and factual. A clear-cut 'these are all the facts you need to know' approach tends to pay particular dividends.

■ *Use captions:* for documents where this is relevant, while pictures, illustrations, photographs and charts can often be regarded as speaking for themselves, they will have more impact if used with a caption. (This can be a good way of achieving acceptable repetition, with a mention in the text and in the caption.)

■ *Use repetition:* key points can appear more than once, for example in a leaflet and an accompanying letter, and even more than once within a letter itself. This applies, of course, especially to benefits repeated for emphasis.

■ *Keep changing the language:* get yourself a thesaurus. You need to find numbers of ways of saying the same thing to create emphasis, for instance in linked documents like a brochure and an accompanying letter.

■ *Say what is new:* assuming you have something new, novel – even unique – to say, make sure the reader knows it. Real differentiation can often be lost, so within the totality of a message make sure that the key points still stand out.

■ *Address the recipient:* you must do this accurately and precisely. You must know exactly to whom you are writing, what their needs, likes and dislikes are and be ever conscious of tailoring the message. Going too far towards being all things to all people will dilute the effectiveness to any one recipient.

■ *Keep them reading:* consider breaking sentences at the end of a page so that readers have to turn over to complete the sentence. (Yes, it does not look quite so neat, but it works.) Always make it clear that other pages follow, putting 'continued…' or similar at the foot of pages as necessary.

■ *Link paragraphs:* this is another way to keep people reading. Use 'horse and cart' points to carry the argument along. For example, one paragraph starts, 'One example of this is…'; the next starts, 'Now let's look at how that works…'.

■ *Be descriptive:* really descriptive. In words, a system may be better described as 'smooth as silk' rather than 'very straightforward to operate'. Remember, *you* know how good what you are describing is, the readers do not. You need to tell them and you must not assume they will catch your enthusiasm from a brief phrase.

■ *Involve people:* first, your people. Do not say 'the head of our XYZ Division', say 'John Smith, the head of our XYZ Division'. And other people. Do not say 'It is a proven service…', say 'more than 300 clients have found it valuable…'.

■ *Add credibility:* for example, if you quote users, quote names (with their permission); if you quote figures, quote them specifically and mention people by name: 'Mary will check this for you.' Being specific adds to credibility, so do not say 'This is described in our booklet on…', rather 'This is described on page 16 of our booklet on…'.

■ *Use repetition:* key points can appear more than once. This applies, of course, especially to benefits repeated for emphasis. You will notice this point is repeated, either to show that the technique works or perhaps to demonstrate that I am pushing a half-hearted attempt at humour too far! If the latter, then it is not to be recommended.

Examples: persuasion within and without the organisation

Here we focus on two examples to illustrate some of the specific different circumstances in which persuasion is necessary. These are: an internal, department-to-department communication and a letter to (potential) customers.

Internal persuasive communication

Consider a short scenario to set us up with an example. Mr B runs the sales office for a medium-sized company. His team is efficient. It comprises people who take customer enquiries, offer technical advice, handle queries of all kinds and take orders (a situation perhaps replaced in too many organisations by the ubiquitous call centre). Recent reorganisation has resulted in the merging of two departments. His people now occupy a large office together with another group: the order processing staff, people dealing with invoicing and documentation. For the most part, all is going smoothly. However, the routing of incoming telephone calls has become chaotic. The switchboard, despite having a note explaining who handles customers in which area of the country, is putting two out of three calls through to the wrong person, and the resulting confusion is upsetting staff and customers alike as calls have to be transferred.

Mr B knows he must sort this out. He carefully drafts and sends a memo to the Personnel Manager, to whom the switchboard operators report, complaining that the inefficiency of their service is upsetting customers and putting the company at risk of losing orders. The memo he e-mailed is shown below.

To: Ms X, Personnel Manager
From: Mr B, Sales Office Manager
Subject: Customer Service

A recent analysis shows that, since the merging of the sales office and order processing departments, two out of three incoming calls are being misrouted by the switchboard and have to be transferred.

This wastes time and, more important, is seen by customers as inefficient. As the whole intention of this department is to hold and develop customer business by ensuring prompt, efficient service, this is not only a frustration internally, it risks reducing customers' image of the organisation and, at worst, losing orders.

> I would be grateful if you could have a word with the supervisor and operators on the switchboard to ensure that the situation is rectified before serious damage results.

He is surprised to find that, far from the situation improving, all he gets is a defensive reply stating the total volume of calls with which the hard-pressed switchboard has to cope, and quoting other issues as being of far greater importance at present to the Personnel department. It concludes by suggesting that he takes steps to ensure customers ask for the right person. Mr B intended to take prompt action that would improve customer service, he felt he had stated his case clearly and logically, yet all he succeeded in doing was rubbing up a colleague the wrong way. The problem remained.

Think, for a moment, of how else this might be handled before reading on. Why did it not work and cause resentment? And what might better have been said?

Here this initial communication was in writing. The e-mail Mr B sent, though well-intentioned, had the wrong effect, and would also have made any follow-up conversation (necessary because the problem had still to be resolved) more difficult.

The problem is certainly identified in the e-mail, the implications of it continuing are spelt out, and a solution – briefing of the relevant staff by the Personnel Manager – is suggested. The intention, as has been said, is good. However, despite a degree of politeness ('I would be grateful...'), the overall tone of the message is easy to read as a criticism. Further, the solution is vague: tell them what exactly? It seems to be leaving a great deal to Personnel. Maybe he felt 'it is not my fault, they should sort it out'. To an extent this may be true, but you may find you often have to choose between a line that draws attention to such a fact and one that sets out to get something done. These are often two different things, and the latter calls for a persuasive approach.

In this case the key objective is to change the action, and to do so quickly before customer relations are damaged. This is more important than having a dig at Personnel, and worth taking a moment over to get the message exactly right. It is, whilst a matter of overall company concern, something of more immediate concern to the sales office.

So what should Mr B have done? To ensure attention, collaboration and action, his message needed to:

▪ make the problem clear;
▪ avoid undue criticism, or turning the matter into an emotive issue;
▪ spell out a solution, or at least a suggestion of one;
▪ make that solution easy and acceptable to people in Personnel (and, not least, the switchboard operators themselves).

Perhaps with that in mind, he should have written something more like the following.

To: Ms X, Personnel Manager
From: Mr B, Sales Office Manager
Subject: Customer Service

The recent merger of the sales office and order processing departments seems to have made some problems for the switchboard.

You will find that I have set out in this note something about what is happening and why, and offer specific suggestions to put it right. You will see the suggested action is mainly mine, but I would like to be sure that you approve before proceeding.

The problem
Since the merger, two out of every three incoming calls are misrouted and have to be transferred. This wastes time both in my department and on the switchboard and is, of course, also likely to be seen as inefficient by customers. To preserve customer relations, and perhaps ultimately prevent orders being lost, the problem needs to be sorted out promptly.

The reason

Apart from the sheer volume of calls, always a problem at this time of the year, the problem is one of information. The switchboard operators have insufficient information to help guide them, and what they do have has been outdated by the departmental merger. Given clear guidance neither they, nor customers, will have any problems.

Action

What I would suggest, therefore, are the following actions:

1. I have prepared a note (and map) showing which member of staff deals with customers from which geographic area, and would like to make this available for reference on the switchboard.
2. This might be best introduced at a short briefing meeting. If we could assemble the operators for 10 minutes before the board opens one morning, I could go through it with them and answer any questions.
3. Longer term, it would be useful if the operators visited our department and saw something of what goes on. We could arrange a rota and do this over a few lunch hours so that it can be fitted in conveniently and without loss of productivity (we'll provide some sandwiches!).

If this seems a practical approach, do let me know and I will put matters in hand.

This is not set out as the sole 'right' or guaranteed approach, but it is certainly different and, I believe, better. And it is more likely to work because it is designed specifically to be persuasive. Note especially that it:

■ lays no blame;
■ recognises that both Personnel and the switchboard are important;
■ considers their needs – for clear guidance, being able to handle the volume of calls more easily, someone else taking the action;

- anticipates objections, Personnel wondering 'Who will do all this?' for instance and their not wanting any hassle;
- is specific in terms of action, who will do what and when (though maybe it could have specified the timing more precisely).

There seems every chance it will have the desired effect. Many situations exhibit similar characteristics. All it needs is a clear, systematic approach that recognises the other person's point of view, and *sells* the desired solution and action.

External customer communication

Here is another 'before and after' example, this time initiating contact. It is from a security company to the prospective new owner of a new-build house (addressed to me just before I moved). People moving house provides a good sales opportunity. People are often somewhat dilatory about security, but maybe the pleasure of a new house is likely to make thoughts of making it secure easier to sow.

The first letter is typical. But because it is introspective, features-oriented, containing too much unexplained jargon and formula 'office-speak', it ends up selling itself short and makes an insufficient case out of what should be a strong one. It also has a real clichéd ending and leaves the initiative with the recipient to come back to them, rather than retaining the initiative.

Dear Mr Forsyth,

I understand that you have bought the house on Plot 28 at Saltcote Maltings.

As part of their service the developer has retained us as advisors on all aspects of security including:

- intruder alarm systems;
- security lighting;
- closed-circuit television;

- entryphones;

- any special security problems you may have.

I am writing to introduce my company and to offer our services in regard to security for your new home.

We are dedicated to promoting and performing to high standards and to demonstrate our commitment, we:

- are members of British Security Industry Association;

- have NACOSS (National Approval Council for Security Systems) certification;

- adhere to BS 4737 for equipment installation;

- have ISO 9002 (quality management system) certification.

Enclosed are illustrations of typical robust and unobtrusive equipment we use. An alarm system would normally comprise of a central control unit, keypad to set the system, PIRs (detection units), magnetic door contacts, alarm sounder and panic buttons.

You also have the option to enhance the protection and peace of mind provided by the system through connection to a central monitoring station. The monitoring station operates 24 hours a day, 365 days a year and can alert the police, a key-holder or anyone you specify. There are two options for connection to a central station – Red Care or Digital Communicator.

We can provide an annual maintenance and service contract which includes access to a 24 hour a day call-out service.

For further information please contact me on the above telephone number or complete and return the request form.

We assure you of prompt and diligent service.

Yours faithfully

....

As well as points referred to ahead of the letter, the punctuation and layout could perhaps be improved. So too could the clarity. The objective being set here is clearly to set up a meeting (on site). I think something along the following lines would have made me think better of them – and made a response more likely.

Dear Mr Forsyth,

28 Saltcote Maltings – keeping your new home safe

You must be excited about your planned move. It is a wonderful location which, as formal security advisors to the developer, we are getting to know well.

Sadly any home may be vulnerable these days. And even a cursory glance at crime statistics gives us all pause for thought. No one wants the upset, loss, damage and feeling of fear a break-in produces; however, a little care can reduce risks dramatically.

What better time to check that security arrangements are satisfactory than as you move into a new home? You will want your house, possessions and family to be safe, and we can offer sound advice on just how prudent action can make that so.

It may well be that even minor additions to the standard house specification can improve security significantly, and add a feeling of well-being. You can receive practical, expert advice – whether that is to fit just one more lock, or involves a full range of equipment such as intruder alarms, security lights, an entry-phones or a full 24-hour monitoring service.

You will want to be sure any such advice is just that – sure.

We take our responsibilities, for both recommendation and installation, very seriously. Not only are we members of the British Security Industry Association, we also have NACOSS (National Approval Council for Security Systems) certification and adhere to other quality standards. These associations ensure we keep technically right up to date and are able to offer the best solutions to our customers.

Sound advice
Some of the equipment we use is described in the enclosed brochures. But our first concern is to identify and match your individual requirements, and recommend whatever suits you best.

You can arrange for a visit and discuss matters in principle without any commitment; we will never over-engineer the solution, and will only offer practical recommendations (not least to match your insurer's requirements). You can contact me at once and arrange a meeting; otherwise I will call you soon to see how we may be able to help.

Good security follows sound advice – and saying *it will never happen to us* is really just not one of the options.

Yours sincerely

....

PS. Talk to us in good time – installation done as a new house is completed can ensure wiring is hidden and avoid mess after you move in.

Again this is I think better, both in terms of what it says and how it says it; the punctuation, readability and layout are better too. Both these letters were sent – indeed they were designed to be sent – with brochures. It is impossible to illustrate a whole brochure here, but a few comments are pertinent (see Chapter 7 on longer documents).

As an example of a good explanatory and persuasive letter, one used by the publishers of this book is reproduced here; such a letter could be sent either as a kind of fact sheet, or personalised to make it a real letter. Incidentally, for anyone of an appropriate age, *The Good Non Retirement Guide* is an excellent publication.

"An excellent publication and a very useful guide for retiring officers."

Karen Daft, Personnel Manager, West Midlands Police Authority

<u>Your annual order for *The Good Non Retirement Guide.*</u>
<u>Prices frozen at 2007 edition prices</u>

As someone who's bought previous editions of *The Good Non Retirement Guide,* I wanted to tell you personally that the new 2008 edition is out now. Having previously purchased this book you already know that *The Good Non Retirement Guide* shows that retirement is not so much the end of a career, as the gateway to many exciting new prospects. Now in its 22nd annual edition, the guide is still widely acclaimed as the most informative, lively and authoritative book of its kind.

<u>The 2008 edition is full of updated material</u>

You'll be pleased to hear that the 2008 edition has been completely revised and updated to include the latest information on tax, pensions, investment options, state benefits and consumer rights as well as dozens of new opportunities from paid jobs to leisure activities. The 16 chapters cover:

- Looking Forward to Retirement
- Money in General
- Investment
- Pensions
- Voluntary work
- Holidays

- Leisure
- Tax
- Starting Your Own Business
- Looking for Paid Employment
- Financial Advisors

- Caring for Elderly Parents
- Wills
- Budget Planner
- Health
- Your Home

Up to 30% discount if you purchase multiple copies

Another value-added benefit is that the 2008 edition of *The Good Non Retirement Guide* has been frozen at last year's price – just £16.99. If you wish to purchase multiple copies we can offer you the following generous discounts:

10 – 25 copies SAVE 10%   26 – 50 copies SAVE 15%
51 – 100 copies SAVE 20%   101 – 750 copies SAVE 25%
751 – 5,000 copies SAVE 30%

Plus, we have generously limited post and packing costs to just £2.50 – no matter how many copies you purchase.

I hope what you've read above has whetted your appetite for *The Good Non Retirement Guide*. I'll call you shortly to confirm your annual order. In the meantime, I enclose a brochure, which gives you more details about the book.

Frances Kay
Editor, *The Good Non Retirement Guide*

P.S. Remember, The Good Non Retirement Guide *is the perfect leaving gift for your retiring staff. All prices frozen at 2007 prices!*

A surprising number of documents in fact have some element of persuasion amongst their intentions. They will only act to prompt agreement if the case they put over is well designed to do just that.

5

Matching style to method

Words are chameleons, which reflect the colour of their environment.

Learned Hand

First here – a question: one with a message in mind. Are you sure you should be writing? Not every message is best passed in writing. Would you think it appropriate to hear that you had been made redundant – or better, promoted – in an e-mail? Probably not. Some messages are fine in writing. Others can need more than that: for example, a manager promoting someone might tell them in a one-to-one meeting, but confirm it in writing and send out news about it more widely so that others know what is going on.

The first question

So, the first question to be asked is always about how to communicate. What is appropriate? This is especially true of e-mail. Nothing has contributed more to a reduction in thought about how to communicate in writing than e-mail. It is just so easy to open an inbox and, faced with a long list of messages, dash off replies, only to discover later that what was sent was ill-considered. This can get you into real trouble: something being misunderstood can cause problems – minor or major – and, at worst, something like an angry response can lead to a reprimand or even dismissal. The moral is to take care. Think, and then, having decided on the communication method to be used, think again about the message you send; in context here, think about what you write.

What you do write will be influenced by certain factors relating to the form of what you do. Anything may need an individual approach: here a number of particular methods and tasks are reviewed as examples of matching what is written to the style and purpose of what is to be done. There are of course innumerable possible examples; some are chosen here to span the range. The examples taken are:

■ standard letters;
■ chasing debtors;
■ 'administrative' messages;
■ press releases.

Beyond that, e-mails have their own chapter (Chapter 6), persuasive ones too (Chapter 4), and longer documents – reports and so on – are dealt with in Chapter 7.

Remember: any written business document must stand up to analysis and, as has been said, its only real test is whether its readers find it does the job it was intended to do. This means it must have a clear purpose and that what it says, and how it says it, is understandable; indeed, that it exhibits any other characteristic that it needs to meet its specific intention.

This chapter builds on what has been said to date. The examples here are not included in the form of templates to be slavishly copied. I believe, as you will have gathered, that good writing comes from considering each document in its own right and building up your own good habits. Certainly there is no one right way to write anything. A variety of word combinations and styles can be appropriate, but there are some things that must be done in particular ways and there are certainly things to avoid. First, consider that panacea for those not wanting to think about things – the standard letter.

Standard letters

Word processing is a wonderful gift of technology (when I recall writing the first book I ever produced in longhand it hardly seems possible and makes me seem very old). But some of what it makes possible has real dangers. Standard letters are a case in point.

Such letters (and other documents for that matter) save time and money and it may speed up administration, customer service and more to use them. They can be used to answer enquiries, queries or complaints or to follow up prospects; they save time in a big way, so far be it for me to suggest you do not use them. But if you do, then they better be good.

A bad standard letter may go out, unthinkingly, hundreds of times and either fail to create understanding or, at worst, do actual damage; remember the letter delivered under the hotel door mentioned early on. Standard letters should be:

■ carefully created;
■ reviewed regularly (they will not be equally suitable forever);
■ given a sufficiently narrow focus (they cannot be all things to all people, and it is better to have three similar, but different ones, each fitting slightly different situations, than one that fails to do exactly the job you want for anyone);
■ personalised; for example, with a customer's name and details (this must always be correct; on a famous occasion a financial institution sent out thousands of letters without adding the names, but left their internal description in place. They all arrived addressed 'Dear Rich Bastard');
■ varied, at least a little, if necessary *every time* they are used. Changing a few words or adding an extra sentence or paragraph is a small price to pay for getting the letter exactly right.

Most people can spot inappropriate standard text at 50 metres, and they hate it. You have been warned. If you doubt any of this consider something else that may be important to you: your CV. There is no such thing as a standard CV. They need modifying depending on how they are used; to reflect the requirements of a particular job, say. Here the updating and editing of standard text can affect your whole career; so too for the letters you send with CVs.

Chasing debtors

This is included because the awkwardness of writing such letters can blind the writer to what needs to be done. One example I will never forget was a company that used eight standard letters to chase debts. These were sent progressively, and had an increasing tone of severity about them. They were ruined by the fact that each one had the same heading across the top in red: it said 'Final demand'. Only a moment's thought suggests that repeating this over several letters actually creates disbelief rather than credibility.

Such a letter must reflect firm policy. You decide what to do and state it clearly. A first letter may be no more than a reminder. Further down the line there is a need for firmness and you can only say what you truly intend. If you say that in 10 days the matter will be put in the hands of solicitors, then you must do just that. A lengthy reiteration of hope and then empty threats will achieve nothing.

Most people hate chasing overdue accounts, but remember the old maxim: *it is not an order until the money is in the bank.* It is a job that must be done. I have heard of some bizarre ploys like sending a postcard, thus displaying the debt publicly (at least to the postman). More appropriate is a systematic approach that follows up and follows up again. Ideally you need a fixed number of letters, all of which assume the matter has been overlooked accidentally, but lay down firm action. Such a sequence might go as follows (*note:* words in brackets are comments, not part of the letters):

Dear

£1,550–98: overdue since (date)

You may recall receiving our invoice dated 27 November about a month ago itemising the amount due for (state details and attach a copy).

I am writing to you because this payment is overdue. Perhaps it was simply overlooked, but I would appreciate payment being made promptly (adding details of how payment may be made). If there is any reason other than oversight why this has not been paid, please call (number) and ask to speak to Susan Jones, who will be pleased to discuss the matter with you.

Yours

Dear

£1,550–98: overdue since (date)

My accountant is now pressing me very hard to get this payment in. Very few customers seem to be as forgetful about payment as you appear to have been. Perhaps I may ask that a cheque is sent by return (again you may want to spell out alternative methods of payment, perhaps also restating the credit terms).

Prompt payment will save additional costs for us both, since I am now required to pass the matter over to a collection service if I do not hear from you, with your payment, within seven days.

If there is any problem you want to discuss, please telephone (number) and ask to speak to Susan Jones, who will make every effort to sort matters out.

Yours

Dear

£1,550–98: collection arrangements

I have now written to you a number of times (you might specify) about this payment which dates back to (date) when our invoice clearly specified 30 day payment terms. As I have consistently received no reply, this matter is – as noted in my last letter – now being passed over to a collection service. This will quickly involve you in legal costs.

I do hope that you are able to respond immediately and prevent this. Payment may be made by (list methods).

Yours

The intention here is to be reasonable, clear and invoke the letter of the law (people do after all know that whatever they have contracted for must be paid for). At the end of the day you must rule a line, write no more and put the matter on a legal footing. *Note:* once a threat has been made and does not materialise, most bad payers will infer they have even longer to bolster their own cash flow situation.

Incidentally, this is not a task that can be exclusively carried out through correspondence. Other means of communication may also be involved. One tip: if you also have to telephone, make the call not sitting at your desk, but standing up. It may sound silly, but it works. It stops you saying 'I'm sorry to worry you, but perhaps...' and helps you be far more assertive; if you don't believe it, try it! Sorry, I digress. Such letters are a further good example of the need for planning: what you intend to achieve dictates the words that it makes sense to use.

'Administrative' letters

Clearly there are thousands of things that could come under this heading. Many seem routine; yet can still cause problems. Let us look at an example, one that certainly is routine: a letter from a training organisation to someone who failed to attend a programme on the date on which they were booked for a public course and who wrote requesting a refund.

For such a thing, sounding too formal or adopting an offhand approach, maybe because of urgency or lack of thought, can create letters that do more harm than good; as with this example:

(heading)
15 March 2009

Peter Smith
Clocktower Engineering Ltd
Arlton Road
London N1

Dear Mr Smith,

Thank you for your letter of 14 March. You will see that you missed attending our training programme 'Making Successful Presentations', which you were registered to attend on 10 March because you misread the joining instructions.

The enclosed copy clearly shows that the correct details of time and place were sent to you.

If you want to try again, the programme runs again next month, on 22 April, at the same venue. You will need to record your intention to attend in writing.

Yours sincerely

JOHN NICKSON

This may be accurate, but it is abrupt and is not polite, helpful nor likely to win friends and influence people. How about something along the following lines?

15 March 2009

Peter Smith
Clocktower Engineering Ltd
Arlton Road
London N1

Dear Mr Smith,

Seminar booking for 10 March: 'Making Successful Presentations'

You must have been annoyed to miss attending the above seminar for which you were registered as a delegate; I was sorry to receive your letter of 14 March setting out the circumstances.

In view of the short notice on which you intended to attend, while the joining instructions (copy enclosed) sent to you did give the correct information, we perhaps should have made the details clearer; my apologies.

Luckily the programme is scheduled to run again before too long. I have therefore moved your registration forward to the next date – 22 April. It is at the same venue. I hope you will find this convenient and be able to put the date in your diary now while places remain available. Information about this (and about later dates, just in case) is enclosed.

My secretary, Sue, will telephone you in a day or two to see if this suits. Meantime, I am sure you will find the programme useful when you do attend – if you have any special objectives in attending do let us know; we aim to meet participants' needs as individually as possible.

I look forward to meeting you next month.

Yours sincerely

JOHN NICKSON

Better? I think so. Though this example relates only to a simple confusion – by the client – the approach, letting the reader, who is, of course, a customer, down lightly and still offering convenient alternative action, is better and the difference between the two letters is clear.

Forms demanding special approaches

Certain documents need a special approach because of the way they are regarded within the business world and how they are usually experienced. Where such a convention exists it is worth following it, not slavishly necessarily, but carefully – especially when it is the recipients who dictate the format.

As a final example, this time of the kind of thing needing to be undertaken with particular precision, we turn now to a specific item of external communication. Press relations is an important part of the broader technique of public relations (both confusingly abbreviated to PR). An important element of communication with the media is the issuing of press releases: these are precisely written communications designed to prompt a mention of something that can be described as news about an organisation in various media. They are also referred to as news releases.

Press releases demand that certain conventions are complied with; at least editors will pay more attention to them if they do so. These are spelt out below, together with an example of a press release. You should not follow this slavishly: remember that an element of creativity is always necessary and the overriding idea is to ring bells and differentiate each message from those of others competing for the same space.

Writing a press release

The details of composing an effective press release are set out here, checklist style.

There are two, perhaps conflicting, aspects of putting together a press release that will stand a good chance of prompting press mentions. The first is to comply with the 'form' demanded by the newspapers, magazines and other media to which press releases are sent; the second is to differentiate what you say so that it stands out as being of genuine interest from the very large number of press releases received.

Consider the 'form' first:

▧ It should carry the words 'Press (or News) Release' at the top, together with the date, preferably at the top left side of the first page.

▧ If an embargo is necessary (ie a request not to publish before a certain date, to ensure news appears as near as possible simultaneously – as once an item has been in print others will consider it of less interest), it should be clearly stated: 'EMBARGO: not to be published before (time) on (date)'. Use CAPITALS or **bold type** for emphasis.

▧ Also, at the top you need a heading, not too long but long enough to indicate clearly the contents of the press release or to generate interest in it.

▧ Space text out well with wide margins, reasonable gaps between paragraphs and so on. This allows subeditors to make notes on it.

▧ If it runs to more than one page make sure it says 'continued' or similar at the foot of each page; even breaking a sentence at the end of the page will make it more likely people will turn over.

▧ Similarly, to make it absolutely clear that there is no more, many put 'end' at the foot of the last page.

▧ Use newspaper style. Short paragraphs. Short sentences. Two short words rather than one long one.

▧ Keep it brief: long enough to put over the message and on to a second page if necessary, but no more.

▧ The first sentences are crucial and need to summarise as far as possible the total message.

▧ Avoid overt 'plugging' (although that may well be what you are doing). Do not mention names, etc right at the beginning, for example.

■ Try to stick to facts rather than opinions. An accountant saying 'This event is being arranged for all those who are interested in minimising their tax liability', for example, is better than just claiming 'This event will be of great interest to all those wanting to minimise their tax liability'.

■ Opinions can be given, in quotes, and ascribed to an individual. This works well and can be linked to the attachment of a photograph (which should usually be attached as a print and clearly labelled in case it gets separated from the press release, but also with clear indications as to how an electronic version can be e-mailed).

■ Do not overdo the use of adjectives, which can jeopardise credibility.

■ Avoid underlining things in the text (this is used as an instruction in printing to put words underlined in italics).

■ Separate notes to the recipient from the text as footnotes. For example, 'photographers will be welcome' could get printed as part of the story.

■ Never omit from a press release, at the end, a clear indication of from whom further information can be sought and their telephone number, e-mail address and so on (even if this is on the heading of the first page).

■ Make sure finally that it is neat, well typed and presentable and that it lists any/all enclosures. This last may be obvious perhaps, but it is important.

So, how do you make your press release stand out? There are fewer rules here, but two points are certainly worth bearing in mind.

First, do not 'cry wolf'. Save press releases for when you really have a story. If you send a series of contrived releases, there is a danger that a good one among them will be ignored. Secondly, make sure the story sounds interesting and, without overdoing things, be enthusiastic about it. If you are not, why would they be? Perhaps the only good thing in the world that is contagious is enthusiasm.

KOGAN PAGE

PRESS RELEASE

Towards the 26 hour day...

Patrick has a lucid and elegant style of writing which allows him to present information in a way that is organised, focused and easy to apply. (Professional Marketing)

In today's workplace, the increasing pressure to achieve makes time management a vital skill. *Successful Time Management* aims to help people to work efficiently and effectively and get the results they want.

The book sets out proven, practical guidelines and provides the basis for readers to review their own time management and adopt new working practices to improve their productivity and effectiveness. It contains time-saving ideas, practical solutions and checklists, and advice on:

- controlling paperwork;
- getting and staying organised;
- delegating and working with others;
- creating a focus on key issues.

As author Patrick Forsyth says, 'Whether you are under pressure or not good time management will help you reduce time-wasting and interruptions, focus on the priority tasks that lead to success in your job. This is a career skill, one that helps achievers get ahead, so it is not overstating matters to say that consideration of time management practice and adopting good habits can change people's lives. So too then can this book.'

ENDS

About the author

Patrick Forsyth runs *Touchstone Training & Consultancy,* which advises on marketing, management and communications skills. A successful author, his previous business books have included *How to Motivate People, How to Write Reports* *and Proposals* and *Improving Your Coaching and Training Skills* (also published by Kogan Page).

For further information, to request a review copy, or to interview the author:
Please contact Martha Fumagalli
Telephone: 020 7843 1957
Fax: 020 7837 6348
E-mail: mfumagalli@koganpage.com

Notes to the editor:

£8–99 * Paperback * 1007494483422 * 152 pages
Published by Kogan Page on (date)
Available from all good bookshops or direct from the publisher at:

Kogan Page
120 Pentonville Road
London N1 9JN

Tel: 020 7278 0433
Fax: 020 7837 6348
E-mail: orders@lbsltd.co.uk
Or order online: www.koganpage.com

A creative touch

As a final thought, and a plea to approach business writing creatively and sometimes actively avoid conventional language and approaches, consider this.

Sometimes something special is needed to make a powerful impression. A good example of this is the second or third communication in a sequence aiming to chase something down. These can be difficult to compose because you may feel that your best shot has been sent and you wonder 'What can I do next?' Such follow-up communications can:

■ repeat key issues (but must find a different way to say at least some of the message);

■ simply remind (with strong contacts, this may be all that is necessary);

■ offer different action. (For instance, the first communication to a customer says: 'Buy it', the second says: 'Let us show you a sample', or finds some more novel way of continuing the dialogue).

The following example is of the latter of these. It makes the point that sometimes there is little new left to say, just 'It's me again', especially if the proposition is good and the only reason for lack of confirmation is timing or distraction rather than that the recipient (here a customer) is totally unconvinced. If this is the case, the job is to continue to maintain contact, and ultimately to jog them into action, while appearing distinctive or memorable in the process.

This illustrates what I mean. Following writing a short book for a specialist publisher, I was keen to undertake something on another topic for them in the same unique format. Proposing the idea got a generally good reaction, but no confirmation. I wrote and telephoned a number of times. Nothing positive materialised – always a delay or a put off (you may know the feeling!) Finally, while a further message needed to be sent, all the conventional possibilities seemed to be exhausted. So I wrote and sent the following brief message.

Struggling author, patient, reliable (non-smoker), seeks commission on business topics. Novel formats preferred, but anything considered within reason. Ideally 100 or so pages, on a topic like sales excellence sounds good; maybe with some illustrations. Delivery of the right quantity of material – on time – guaranteed. Contact me at the above address/telephone number or meet on neutral ground, carrying a copy of *Publishing News* and wearing a carnation.

Despite some initial hesitation, wondering if it was over the top (this was someone I had only met once), I did send it. I did so on headed paper and by post, feeling that this would have more impact than an e-mail. Gratifyingly the approach was appreciated and confirmation came the following day (and you can now read the result – *The Sales Excellence Pocketbook*, Management Pocketbooks). Similarly, the example given earlier about the report of a research study (describing the organisation with the phrase 'an old sofa') makes the same point. Both might never have been sent, yet both worked very well. How many things, I wonder, are deleted to a sucking of teeth as 'not really what I can say', when being a little more bold might work much better.

Sometimes a slightly less conventional approach – and some seemingly non-business writing language – does work well. You should not reject anything other than the conventional approach; try a little experiment and see what it can do for you. On that note let's move on to something with which most people have a love/hate relationship: e-mail.

6

Shorter documents: dos and don'ts of the ubiquitous e-mail

Technology is like a bus. If it goes in the direction you want to go, take it.

Renzo Piano

E-mail is one of the quickest ways of communicating with other people, instantly sending as it does letters, memos, pictures and sounds from one computer to another via the internet on a worldwide basis. There are internal networks too, in larger organisations. The technicalities do not need to concern us here, but the communications implications do; so much so that it deserves its own chapter (though there are certainly points here that apply more widely).

In the working environment, e-mailing is often used as a substitute for other kinds of communication, reducing the incidence of face-to-face meetings. This can be useful: it is possible to conduct meetings, correspond with the whole world and use voice and visual contact without leaving your desk.

But the use of e-mail can be overdone, reducing personal contact to the detriment of relationships and collaboration. It is important to have a balance in terms of different forms of contact. Some large organisations have rules to stop any negative effects: 'No internal e-mails are to be sent on a Thursday', and ensure that people continue to talk face-to-face.

Because e-mailing is so rapid, it puts pressure on people to get it right first time in terms of passing a clear message. There is a tendency to reply fast, to 'dash them off' and not give them much thought. This is a practice that must be resisted.

The attractiveness of e-mailing is without doubt its speed. Mail is sent virtually immediately you click the 'Send' button. Your message should be received very quickly after it is sent. The speed of any reply is then dependent only on how regularly someone checks their e-mail inbox and takes time to reply. The fast to and fro nature of e-mail communication can be positive: prompting rapid action and boosting efficiency.

E-mail versus snail mail

E-mail can be, indeed usually is, less formal than writing a letter. Let me say this firmly and up front: the level of formality must be selected wisely.

There are those to whom you may write very informally (incorporating as many abbreviations, grammatical shortcuts, minimal punctuation and bizarre spellings as you wish) *as long as your meaning is clear*. But others (customers, senior colleagues) may resent this or think worse of you for it. Sometimes (often? usually?) an e-mail must be as well written as any important letter. It is safest to adopt a fairly formal style, and certainly a clear one, and to err on the side of more rather than less formality if you are unsure. You have been warned! Proofreading and spell checking is as important here as with many other documents.

The main purpose of e-mail is not for lengthy communications but usually for short, direct giving or gathering of information. Lengthy e-mails are difficult to read and absorb on screen. For this and other reasons, alternative means of communication are sometimes better selected (or an e-mail may have a hard copy sent on). Longer information can be added as a Word document attached to an e-mail, but you need to have confidence that someone will take time to check and see it as sufficiently important to do so. Ditto their printing it out. Never forget just how easy it is to ignore an e-mail. Click; and it is gone in a spilt second – and for ever.

When replying to an e-mail, you don't have to worry about finding the sender's name and address and job title. Replying only involves the pressing of a button and their address appears in the top left-hand box of the reply page. It is possible to keep the copy of their sent message on the page, so that you can refer to it when replying.

As an example of what is possible, a company located in Wisconsin in the United States e-mailed its service consultants in Cambridge, in the United Kingdom, about obtaining a specific part for a processing machine. The UK office e-mailed the manufacturers in Manila, in the Philippines, for information. They responded by e-mail within minutes. The reply was then transmitted back to the US company. The total time taken was 17 minutes to circumnavigate the world and deliver what was regarded as exceptional service.

E-mail: possible disadvantages

E-mail is not universally wonderful. For instance:

- It is obviously impossible to communicate with someone electronically unless the recipient has a computer set up to receive e-mail, and is near it or near another machine that will allow access over the internet.
- E-mail agreement is just as legally binding as a formal document; treating it otherwise can cause problems.
- Technical problems may put your system out of action, and technical back up needs to be in place (it is not a question of if it happens, but when).

■ Most junk e-mail – or 'spam' – is just as irritating as the junk mail that arrives through the letterbox. The responsibility rests with the user and it is sensible to reduce its volume by having, and keeping up to date, software that isolates it (though some always seems to slip through).

■ Caution should be exercised in opening e-mails and attachments from unknown recipients, as viruses, Trojan horses and worms can invade the computer system if care is not taken; more on this later.

Enough has been said already about e-mail for other problems to be apparent. People sending personal messages can waste much time in an organisation. If this is done on a company heading or format there may be legal implications too; what happens if something is libellous? Thus organisations need a firm policy and guidelines and everyone needs to be disciplined in following the rules about writing this way.

Some basic guidelines

As has been said, e-mails can be more informal than letters, but certain criteria as regards style and content are sensible (again an organisation may set out guidelines). Given the volume of e-mails people receive, you are competing for attention and must compose e-mails that are effective. An e-mail should be:

■ *brief* – use plain words;
■ *direct* – clear presentation, no ambiguity;
■ *logical* – with a clear structure.

Whether e-mails are being sent internally or externally, as a substitute for a letter or not, it is important to ensure these rules are observed. A clear heading will make its purpose apparent and it may also be helpful to flag any (real!) urgency and say whether, and perhaps when, a reply is sought.

Remember that e-mail can, like any communication, have many intentions – to inform, persuade, etc.

Before sending an e-mail, considering the following will help ensure that it is presented effectively:

- What is the *objective* or purpose of the e-mail? Do you know what you are trying to achieve? Is the e-mail a request for information? Are you circulating standard information? If the e-mail is a quick response to a query, make sure that what you say is correct. If you are unsure, explain that this is an acknowledgement of receipt, and you will come back with more as soon as you can, preferably saying exactly when. If you do not know what the objective is, think carefully before sending your communication.

- What is the *background* to the issue? Is the reason for sending the e-mail something that is to do with a problem in a project? Is an explanation, excuse or apology required? Is it to elicit more information or to provide detailed answers to a query? For an e-mail to be clearly understood, it must be apparent why you are sending it. If you don't know, check before going into print.

- Who is the intended *recipient*? Will it reach them directly, or be read by another person? E-mail in-boxes are not necessarily only opened by the person named in the 'Send to' box. It is possible that colleagues have access to a person's mailbox, for example when someone is sick or on holiday. It is important to bear this in mind when writing a message in case of problems.

- What *style* are you using? How is it being presented? Is the style really informal? Are you replying to a message that was half-encrypted with lots of missing capital letters, text message-style shortened words, emoticons, etc? If so, that is fine. But think carefully what impression the style of the e-mail gives to someone who is opening a communication from you for the first time or who thinks of you in a particular way.

- Choice of *content*. What is the e-mail saying and is it being clearly communicated without any vagueness and ambiguity? If the e-mail covers complex matters, it may be better to explain that a document follows. It is usually intended for e-mails to be read quickly, and the content should reflect this.

■ Is there a *conclusion*/recommendation/response required? If so, is this obvious? It may be clearest to place any request for action at the end of the e-mail. Also by saying something like 'It would be helpful if you could bring this information with you when we meet at 4 pm', you give the recipient a clear message that they have until 4 pm to complete the task. Finishing off an e-mail with a direct instruction, or repeating the purpose of the message, will leave the reader in no doubt of your intention.

■ What, if any, *attachments* are being sent? Specify any attachments clearly. If a device is used to 'squash' information together – such as zip files, it is always helpful to explain what system you use. If the attachments require certain software to open them, explain what is needed. This is particularly important where graphics and images are being sent. Some of these attachments can take ages to download and it is helpful to say so.

Putting yourself across appropriately in an e-mail is important, because it is instant and non-retrievable. As with other written communication, there is no tone of voice, facial expression, posture, body language or gestures to augment your message. As e-mail is a rapid and concise form of communication, the detail matters (see box).

Getting the detail right

These are some of the most important points of detail to remember:

■ *Format* – use an appropriate format or house style – this is often available as a template. Make sure it matches the style used in the company's letters and faxes and check what other aspects of layout you are expected to conform to.

- *Typography/font* – most companies have a prescribed font and style but others can be chosen from the drop-down list box. The screen shot shows the font and size selected. You can also select the option to point up text in your e-mail, using devices such as **bold**, <u>underline</u> and *italic*. And remember that reading on screen is not as easy as from paper – so make sure your chosen typeface is legible.

- *Subject* – writer reference, case number or project name. This is just a polite way of ensuring that the recipient can save time by reading what the e-mail refers to. If you are sending an e-mail to someone about a particular matter, it is helpful if they understand immediately what the message is about.

- *Salutation* – are you on first name terms? Do you need to write in more formal style because you have not exchanged correspondence before? Do you know the name of the person to whom you are writing or must you use an impersonal salutation?

- *Punctuation* – beware ambiguity. A missing comma or no full stop can often cause confusion. It may be 'cool' amongst some people to lose capitals and miss out dots and dashes, but if the reader is left puzzled by the meaning, you are less likely to get a useful exchange of information.

- *Line length* – short sentences and line length make for easier reading on screen. This is explained in more detail further on. Do not use complex sentences or syntax. Short and sweet is best.

- *Paragraphing* – options are available from the drop-down list, including headings, bulleted and numbered lists. Paragraphing should be used where there is a change of topic or subject, so that the reader is aware that a new point is being introduced.

- *Consistency* – if the e-mail contains numbering, take care. It is extremely irritating if the numbering changes in style or is inconsistent. If you are making a number of points, stick to a) b) c) or 1.i, 1.ii, 1.iii or whatever style or format you prefer.

- *Valediction* – unlike a formal letter you don't have to sign off 'Yours faithfully' or 'Yours sincerely'; however, in some cases it may be appropriate to end with an informal sign off. Many people use 'Kind regards', 'Many thanks' and 'Best wishes', or more impersonally, though with a few less key strokes every time, 'Yours'.

■ *Details of the writer* – title, company. With e-mails it is possible to set all this up as a 'default' signature, which appears at the foot of the message. This includes your name and title as well as details of the company you represent (you don't want someone trying to reply to you and finding your phone number is not there).

■ *Contact details* – these go with the signature and should include any contact details necessary – as above.

■ *Attachments* – as mentioned before, these should be clearly described and mentioned in the text. If they are in different format, such as PDF files, it is a good idea to ensure beforehand that the recipient's computer is able to receive these files in readable form.

Note: While these points are especially important in the context of the special nature of e-mail, they overlap with the general principles of what makes any written message effective, dealt with earlier.

Digital signatures and other security devices

Several other things should be noted with regard to security:

■ *Electronic signatures* are being used more widely as more people send information by e-mail. In addition, it is more important than ever that e-mails cannot be read by anyone other than your recipient. By using digital IDs or signatures you can ensure that no one is pretending to be you and sending false or misleading information under your name. Digital IDs in Outlook Express can prove your identity in electronic transactions, rather like producing your driving licence when you need to prove your identity. Digital IDs can also be used to encrypt (code) e-mails to keep the wrong people from reading them. Digital IDs are obtained from independent certification authorities whose websites contain a form which, when completed, contains your personal details, and instructions on installing the digital ID. This is used to identify e-mails and ensure the security of your messages.

■ *Encryption* is a special way to send sensitive information by e-mail. It is a form of electronic code. One code is used to encrypt the message and another code is used to decrypt it. One key is private, and the other is public. The public key is passed to whoever needs to use it, whether they are sending the message (in which case they would use it for encryption) or are receiving the e-mail (in which case they would use it to decrypt the message). There is a wide range of information that you might consider disguising in this way, ranging from an account number to the fact that your company is launching a radical new product on a certain date.

■ *Records:* some e-mail systems allow a note to be shown when an e-mail has been sent, received, opened and read by the recipient. This can be important in some time-critical instances. Alternatively, just ask for an acknowledgement. This is obviously key when deadlines are involved; I always ask for acknowledgement when submitting material for an article or book.

E-mail files can become very important. Losing them can be a disaster. It is advisable, therefore, *to regularly back up* your files and company data to safeguard against such risks. If passwords are used in your computer system, consider changing them on a regular basis to stop hackers and avoid misappropriation.

There may be company guidelines about this, indeed about backing up your whole computer; but the responsibility for implementation is often likely to be personal.

'E-mailspeak' – the role of language

We have already touched on the lack of formality of many e-mail messages. But clarity is essential and many messages must look and sound good, and over-informality can dilute professionalism. So, remember to spellcheck your e-mails when necessary. Be aware of easily confused words and use the computer's spellchecker with caution. For example, how easily a sentence's meaning is changed by the substitution of a simple word. Consider a message saying 'After further consideration I have decided that your request for a salary increase of £10,000 per annum will now be agreed.' Try that sentence again inserting the word 'not' instead of 'now'.

Similarly, use grammar and language checks and such features as the Thesaurus: all help produce an effective message. It is possible to select alternative words or phrases to avoid confusion when using the grammar check tool.

There is a good deal elsewhere in this book about pure writing skills, so suffice it to say here that you should avoid:

- *over-complexity* ('from time to time' instead of 'occasionally', 'it is necessary that' instead of 'must');
- *tautology* or unnecessary repetition ('new innovation', 'close proximity' and 'postpone until later');
- *unnecessarily long words* ('anticipate' instead of 'expect', 'requirement' instead of 'need');
- *overlong sentences*.

All such things make the essentially simple e-mail unwieldy and less likely to do a good job.

Jargon and acronyms

Let's face it, everything seems to attract abbreviations. Writers say that I am at the BOSHOK stage of writing this book – bum on seat, hands on keyboard. E-mails particularly seem to attract abbreviations. Those containing jargon, text language and acronyms (where initial letters are used to make up another word) are more likely to be confusing. However, because of e-mail's overriding informality it is a good idea to be familiar with those that are universally used. There are many around and new ones are springing up daily, not least due to the popularity of text messaging. Here is a selection of some of the more common acronyms that you are likely to see in e-mails:

AFAIK	As far as I know
BCNU	Be seeing you
BTW	By the way
CUL8R	See you later
FYI	For your information
TNX	Thanks

It would be a good idea to learn these and any additional ones that are commonly used within your company, profession or industry sector. Beware using them in e-mails that are being sent externally, where the recipient may not understand them; it is sometimes courteous to use full terminology in parenthesis afterwards.

Attachments

E-mail is made infinitely more useful because documents and files can be attached to messages. Attachments can include word-processed documents, images, sound or video files. It is even possible to e-mail computer programs.

When an attachment is sent the e-mail program copies the file from where it is located and attaches it to the message. Image files can take some time to upload and download, so it is advisable to keep these to a minimum if speed is of the essence.

Sometimes it may help to compress files that are being sent as e-mail attachments. This will reduce the upload time while transmitting the information. It also speeds up the download time for you if someone sends you a large file that has already been zipped. 'Zip' and 'Stuff it' are well-known programs and Microsoft Windows includes a compression tool in its latest version.

The advantage of sending documents and files as attachments is the speed and efficiency of communication. The recipient of the documents will be able to keep these on file and can move, edit, return or forward them on as necessary.

If security is an issue, an attachment should be sent as a PDF (Portable Document Format). This format prevents the document being edited by the recipient. This is a security device and the document can be printed off but not amended. This is very safe and secure for sensitive material.

Hyperlinks

Inserting hyperlinks into e-mail messages is particularly useful when sending information to people. If something that you do not have a copy of but which is available on a web page needs to be communicated to your recipient, insert the hyperlink into the e-mail message. The recipient simply clicks on the link and this action opens the web page. Remember doing this takes time and some people may not bother; for instance, information sent this way to a customer as a part of a total message might never be seen, diluting the whole effect. It is, however, a good way to enhance technical information.

Potential problems

E-mail, and the internet on which it is dependent, can pose some serious problems: spam, viruses and the time-wasting inherent in managing e-mail files inefficiently, are familiar to us all and this is not the place to list details and remedies (though it is worth saying that care is necessary and guidelines within an organisation about security, etc should be followed strictly). However, let's end this chapter with a few dos and don'ts and points that go a little beyond the writing of these electronic messages.

Don't

- Send e-mails just because they are easy.
- Enter text IN CAPITAL LETTERS. It is taken as shouting.
- Use e-mails as a substitute for properly delegating a task to another.
- Send them to discharge yourself of responsibility.
- Put something in an e-mail that is confidential; it can be abused.
- Forward someone's e-mail without their permission.
- Assume your recipient wanted it and is desperate to receive it.

Do

- Think and read before sending anything (or use the 'send later' button to inject some thinking time).
- Be precise to eliminate follow-up checks and phone calls.
- Reply promptly. Because e-mail is quick, a reply is generally expected sooner rather than later.
- Be polite and friendly but never assume familiarity with jargon.
- Keep attachments to a minimum.
- Avoid gobbledygook.

Overall, the message here is simple. Use technology for written messages where it benefits you, but do so carefully – recognise any downsides and make sure that attention to detail makes what you do effective. Remember that you can tell a lot about a person from their 'e-mail exterior'. An e-mail can provide a window to someone's status in the workplace, work habits, stress levels and even their personality. For example, managers who send e-mails tend to use 'higher status' techniques. They usually use a greater level of formality and tone and you will rarely see cheesy quotes, smiley faces (emoticons) or joke mails.

E-mails are a valuable modern communication tool for us all, but if abused or used carelessly, they can cause trouble. In summary, here are 10 basic tips for better e-mail technique:

1. *Use e-mail as one channel of communication, but not the only one.* This is important: do not be lazy just because it is fast and easy. E-mails can document discussions and send high-impact messages around the world at the click of a mouse. But they can also mislead managers into thinking they can communicate with large groups of people solely through regular group e-mails. Use e-mail widely but only as one of a range of management tools. It is not possible to reach everyone, and the 'impersonal' non-direct contact means that people can feel slighted by the loss of the personal touch.

2. *It pays to keep it short and sweet.* E-mails that are longer than a full screen tend not to be read straight away. They get left till later and often not until the end of the day or beyond. It is important to judge when it is right to put down the mouse and seek the person out face to face, or pick up the phone and speak to them.

3. *Communicate clearly – cut out the codes.* E-mail requires clarity of purpose. Be sure your message comes across without any doubt or misunderstanding. Also it is important to be sure to whom your message needs to be addressed, and who – really – needs a copy for information. In terms of actions and priorities, use lists or bullet points for clarity. Response buttons (or similar) should be used if you need to see who has received and read your message.

4. *To encourage open communication* when using e-mail, request people to respond with questions or queries if they wish. It shows that you are concerned and available to help.

5. *Do not use e-mails to get mad at people.* Far better to save anger for face-to-face encounters (where facial expression and body language can be used to great effect) or over the phone where tone of voice can speak volumes. Sarcasm, irony, criticism or venom is not appropriate when sending e-mails. Certainly it is difficult to project such feelings clearly, and messages can come over as far more harsh than you intended.

6. *Humour should be used with caution.* By all means use wit and humour to lighten a heavy atmosphere, but emoticons, smiley faces and joke e-mails are not usually appropriate in the work environment. If being facetious is usual for you, it may make it more difficult to strike a serious note when you need to. Some companies ban joke e-mails; they are too risky and may erode your attempts to send serious ones.

7. *Suspend reaction – use the five-minute rule.* It is often wise to delay sending a hastily written e-mail for five minutes (or more!). If you are angry or upset when you write something, it is a good idea either to take a break or go for a walk or do something else, before writing. Once you have cooled off, take a moment to review your message before pressing the 'send' button.

8. *Set aside time to deal with e-mails.* Because of the growing importance of e-mails as a percentage of the total number of messages you receive, you need to make time to deal with them; if this demands reconfiguring your working day – so be it.

9. *Take advantage of language.* To avoid errors and complicated sentences, use words carefully to ensure clarity of communication, which accompanies the brevity so beloved of e-mail writers.

10. *Think* about your e-mails and finally do *not* send copies to all and sundry – this is a prime cause of people complaining that they get too many e-mails and that many are unnecessary.

7

Longer documents

> What is written without effort is in general read without pleasure.
>
> *Samuel Johnson*

Long documents present their own problems. Some people might regard 'long' as anything more than two or three pages, while others might reserve this description for report-type documents of 10, 20 or more pages.

Once upon a time my then boss called me into his office (I worked for a medium-sized consulting firm at the time) and asked me if I would write a book – well, told me to, now I think of it! He had just done one successfully and the publisher was asking for more. I remember that my jaw dropped. It seemed an impossible task, but I had to admit that I knew the proposed subject and that I could, as he put it, 'write a page on it'. This agreed, he went on, 'OK, write a page, then write another 149 and you'll have a book.' I did; though the result is safely out of print; it was at that time that I decided I had to learn (a lot) more about writing.

In terms of business writing, however, he had a point. Nothing is that long, not even this book. It is some 40,000 words, but it is divided into seven chapters and each of those (written I hope in an accessible way) addresses numbers of issues and is in turn broken down into a number of sections. If one regards each as an entity, then at one level there are rarely more than two or three thousand words to consider together. Of course, the overall content needs planning and organising, but with a plan in mind the writing falls mainly into bite-sized sections. So too does a report, proposal or any other business document. Regarded this way, all are, in fact, manageable.

Write tight

In a busy life people always say they want something brief, but the word just means 'short'. This should not, in fact, be an end in itself: a better intention is to make things *succinct*, that is short but containing all the essentials to inform in an understandable way. Length should not be artificially extended by things that are not relevant, and you should remember that comprehensiveness is rarely (ever?) an option. If you wrote everything you that you could about anything, most of the content may be superfluous. This means selection is important: you need first to decide what to write and what to omit (see the comments about planning in Chapter 2).

Similarly, writing style also affects length. A convoluted style will fill more pages, and there is an expression to the effect that you should *write tight*. For example, look at the phrase below and see how many words you can abbreviate it to without changing the sense:

> In spite of the fact that he was successful, it did not take him long before he was sorry that he had used so many words.

It is worth taking a minute or two to try this, and then look at a comment about it in the box at the end of this chapter on page 124. Here are two more if you want to see if you get better and better at this kind of editing:

One of the main consequences of rising property values is that it will be more difficult for people to afford new homes. *(22 words)*

John did not pay any attention to the results because he did not have very much confidence in the analytical techniques. *(21 words)*

Note: there is an important balance to be struck here. If you omit salient parts of a case, then meaning and intention may well be diluted – the message is left incomplete and lacks power. Make something too long, however, and people switch off and do not read it all. The answer? If in doubt it is better to write more, provided you are sure that the extra points do improve the likelihood of achieving your intention.

Reports

Here I want to say something about the most common long business documents. These come in many forms: feasibility studies, research reports, staff appraisals and many more. Here we focus on the general principles.

First, the greater the length and/or complexity, the more important it is to prepare carefully: to set clear objectives and focus appropriately on the reader. Similarly, greater length demands a clear structure.

The simplest structure one can imagine is a beginning, a middle and an end. Indeed, this arrangement is what a report must consist of, but the argument or case it presents may be somewhat more complex. For example, imagine a report of an examination of something (a process or new initiative, say) setting out its analysis and recommendations. This may fall naturally into four parts:

1. setting out the *situation*;
2. describing the *implications*;

3. reviewing the *possibilities;*
4. making a *recommendation;*

The two structures can coexist comfortably; the overriding consideration is logic and organisation.

An example helps spell out the logical way an argument needs to be presented if it is to be got over clearly. Imagine an organisation with certain communication problems; a report making suggestions to correct this might follow this broad sequence:

1. *The situation:* this might refer to both the quantity and importance of written communication around, and outside, the organisation. Also to the fact that writing skills were poor, and no standards were in operation, nor had any training ever been carried out to develop skills or link them to recognised models that would be acceptable around the organisation.
2. *The implications:* these might range from a loss of productivity (because documents took too long to create and had to constantly be referred back to clarify), to inefficiencies or worse, resulting from misunderstood communications. It could also include dilution or damage to image because of poor documents circulating outside the organisation, perhaps to customers.
3. *The possibilities:* here, as with any argument, there might be many possible courses of action, all with their own mix of pros and cons. To continue the example, these might range from limiting report writing to a small core group of people, to reducing paperwork completely or setting up a training programme and subsequent monitoring system to ensure some improvement took place.
4. *The recommendation:* here the 'best' option needs to be set out. Or, in some reports, a number of options must be reviewed from which other people can choose. Recommendations need to be specific, addressing exactly what should be done, by whom and when, alongside such details as cost and logistics.

Note: Before reading on, you might cross-check whether these four section descriptions apply to any documents you must write, or whether you can think of more pertinent descriptions to divide up any particular category of report with which you may have to deal regularly. However they are described, bite-sized sections are always needed.

At all stages, generalisations should be avoided. Reports should contain facts, evidence and sufficient 'chapter and verse' for those in receipt of them to see them as an appropriate basis for decision or action.

With the overall shape of the argument clearly in mind you can look in more detail at the shape of the report itself. The way in which it flows through from the beginning to the end is intended to carry the argument, make it easy to follow and to read, and to make it interesting – even surprising and/or memorable – too, as necessary, along the way.

Two special features of reports are useful: appendices and executive summaries. An *appendix* removes material from the main text and places it at the end of a report; this allows the main content to be read without distraction and yet also lets readers check further details as and when they wish. An *executive summary* is a summary in the conventional sense but is put at the beginning of a report (rather than at the end) to provide an overview of what follows; essentially it acts to say *what follows is worth reading.*

Similarly, a long document must look right. It needs adequate space and headings, clear numbering and clear emphasis (this last delivered by graphic devices ranging from *italics* to boxed paragraphs); more of this later.

Proposals

These are a form of report that must also persuade (maybe a customer or a colleague). A proposal that is inadequate in some small detail compared to one from a competitor (and very often your proposal is in competition) may easily be placed second. Your proposal may be rated less impressive or appropriate by only a whisker – but you are still out. So the quality of written proposals is vital. In such situations there are usually no second prizes.

Proposals may vary. Sometimes agreement comes after sending just a page or two of text by e-mail (as was writing this book come to think of it; sorry, I digress). Other things may need substantial documentation as part of the process of gaining agreement. Such a process may be long, costly and multi-staged with proposals playing a sequential part. In other words people can say no to a poor proposal and decide not to move on to complete the process. Because this is harsh, but true, whatever kind of proposal is necessary, it must be done right. First, let us define terms.

Quotations versus proposals

It is worth being clear about what exactly is meant by the two words 'proposal' and 'quotation'. Although they are sometimes used in a way that appears similar, in sales terms they each imply something very different.

Proposals have to explain and justify what they suggest. They normally make recommendations, they certainly should assume that their job is to persuade. On the other hand, quotations are normally much simpler documents. They set out a particular – usually requested – option. They say that something is available and what it costs. They assume, rightly or wrongly, that the sales job is done and that persuasion is not necessary. This may be true, especially in known situations. But many quotations should have more, sometimes much more, of the proposal about them. Here the review is concerned with the more complex proposals, though the principles concerned might also act to beef up any quotations you use and may be useful to other writing tasks too.

Choice of format

There are two main overall approaches to the format of proposals. Sometimes a letter, albeit maybe a longish one, is entirely appropriate. Indeed, sometimes doing more than this can overstate a case and put the recipient off. It is seen as over-engineering. Alternatively, what is necessary is much more like a report, though one with a persuasive bent.

Note: a further form is the *discussion document* – a document for a stage before a proposal is appropriate. Classically this sets the scene for a meeting, dealing with background and defining areas and ideas to be discussed at a meeting. Like all such documentation exactly how it is written is vital to its success. A subsequent proposal, dependent on the discussion document being viewed as good, is thus an extension of this when both are involved.

Let's consider the main forms in turn, and when and why each may be appropriate.

Letter proposals

This is simply what the name suggests. It starts with a first sheet set out like a letter, which begins, 'Dear...'. It may be several pages long, with a number of subheadings, but it is essentially less formal than a report-style proposal. This style is appropriate when:

- a more detailed proposal is not needed, because there would be insufficient content, or an over-formality;
- the objective (or request) is only to summarise discussions that have taken place;
- there are no outstanding issues (unsolved at prior meetings, for instance);
- there is no threat of competition.

Where these, or some of them, do not apply, another approach is safer or necessary.

Formal proposal

This is a report-style document, usually printed and bound in some way and thus more elaborate and formal (colour and illustrations may also be involved). This is appropriate when:

▦ recommendations are complex;
▦ what is being sold (or asked for) is high in cost (or, just as important, will be *seen* as being so);
▦ there is more than one decision maker, a committee, a recommender and a decision maker acting together, or some other combination of people who need to confer and will thus see exactly the same thing;
▦ (linked to the previous one) you have not met some of those who will be instrumental in making the decision;
▦ you know you have competition and are being compared.

One question before we continue. How many copies of a proposal should you send? The short answer is to ask and send however many are requested. In many businesses it is common for there to be multiple decision makers or influencers. Where this is even suspected it is doubly wise to ask how many copies of a proposal will be required. If you have seen, say, two people and the answer is three copies, maybe there is someone else you need to be aware of and more questions (or even another meeting) become the 'order of the day' before you move on. One way or another you have to find out the role any additional people play and make sure that the proposal addresses them as well as others.

In anything to do with persuasion and selling, the readers and their views must naturally rank high. What they want should rightly influence the kind of proposal you submit. Ask people questions such as:

▦ How formal should it be?
▦ What sort of detail is expected?
▦ How long should it be? (I have known cases where vastly longer documents than required have been submitted because this question was not asked.)

■ How many people will see it (as mentioned above)?
■ When do they want to receive it?

You do not have to follow their answers slavishly, but must make a considered judgement. For example, if you are dealing with someone you know, they may well suggest not being too formal. But, if you know you have competition and they are in discussion with other people, it may still pay to do something more formal than a letter; after all your document and someone else's will be compared alongside each other. In a comparison between a letter-style and a more formal proposal, the former tends to look weaker, especially when related to value for money.

Timing

Timing is worth a particular word. It is naturally good to meet people's deadlines, even if in some cases it means 'burning the midnight oil'. However, it is likely that people want your proposal to reflect your *considered* opinion. Promising that on a complex matter in 24 hours may simply not be credible. Too much speed in such a case can cast doubts on quality and originality. This is especially true of anything complex or creative; and when solutions are positioned as being truly bespoke, they range from accountancy to IT systems. In consequence, it may occasionally be politic to delay something, asking for more time than you actually need to enhance the feeling of tailoring and consideration when it arrives. It's good to have time in hand for contingencies too.

So, at this stage you know something about what's needed, you know who is involved in the decision (ie those who will read whatever you write) and when the proposal is wanted. Remember the need for preparation: add in any time that composing such a document demands you spend with colleagues – in discussion, brainstorming, whatever – and set aside sufficient time to do a good writing job. Once the document is sent, then, for good or ill, it must stand on its own feet.

Certainly once something has been sent, you have to live with it. You cannot reasonably telephone a correction later or send a 'revised page 7' to be slotted in by the recipient. With all that in mind, let us now turn to see how the content should be arranged and dealt with within a proposal.

Proposal content and arrangement

While the format and certainly the content of a proposal can vary, the main divisions are best described as:

- the introduction (usually preceded by a contents page);
- the statement of need;
- the recommendations (or solution);
- areas of detail (such as costs, timing, logistics, staffing and technical specification);
- closing statement (or summary);
- additional information (of prime or lesser importance, in the form of appendices).

Each section may need a number of subheadings and their length may vary with context, but they form a convenient way of reviewing the key issues about the construction of a proposal and are thus now commented on in turn:

Title/contents page

A proposal of any complexity needs the equivalent of a book's title page. This states who, or which organisation, it is for, what it is about and who it is from. This page can also give the contact details of whoever it is from (which, if not here, certainly must be somewhere in the proposal) and, on a sales proposal, some people like to feature the logo of the recipient organisation, as well as their own.

This should be followed by a front sheet on which the contents of the proposal are listed and which gives the page numbers. It may make it look more interesting, and easier to navigate both as and after it is read, if there are subheadings as well as main headings, especially if the main headings have to be bland, for instance, 'The introduction' (a term often best avoided or at least added to).

Note: the headings that follow are descriptive of the functions and role of the sections, not recommendations for headings you should necessarily use. These are often better less bland and more descriptive and memorable.

Introduction

Remember that a proposal is a *persuasive* document. The opening must command attention, establish interest and lead into the main text, making people want to read on. As the introduction has to undertake a number of important, yet routine, tasks, ahead of them it may be best to start with a sentence (or more) that is interesting, rings bells with the reader and sets the tone for the document.

Thereafter there are a number of other roles for the introduction. For instance it may need to:

■ establish the background;
■ refer to past meetings and discussions;
■ recap decisions made to date;
■ quote experience;
■ acknowledge terms of reference;
■ list the names of those involved in the discussions and/or preparation of the document.

As none of this is as interesting as what will follow (if it is, then you do have a problem!), this section should concentrate on essentials and be kept short. Its final words should act as a bridge to the next section.

Statement of need

This section needs to set out, with total clarity, the brief in terms of the need: why the proposal is being written. It describes the scope of the requirement, and may well act to recap and confirm what was agreed at a prior meeting about what the proposal would cover.

It is easy to ask why this section should be necessary. Surely someone who has asked for a proposal knows what they want? Indeed they have perhaps just spent a considerable amount of time telling you exactly that. But this statement is still important. Why?

Well, its role is to make clear that *you have complete understanding* of the situation. It emphasises the identity of views between the two parties and gives credibility to your later suggestions by making clear that they are based firmly on the real – and individual – needs that exist. Without this it might be possible for someone to assume that you are suggesting what is best (or perhaps most profitable) for you, or simply making a standard suggestion.

This section is also of key importance if the proposal is to be seen by people who were not party to the original discussions; for them it may be the first clear statement of this picture. Again, this part should link naturally into the next section.

Recommendation or solution

This may well be the longest section and needs to be logically arranged and divided (as do all the sections) to make it manageable. Clear and informative headings are needed. Here you state what approach you feel meets the requirements. This may be: a) standard, in the sense that it is a list of, for example, recommended approaches/products that you have discussed and sell as a standard solution; or b) 'bespoke', for example as with the approach a consultant might set out to instigate a process of change, implement training or indeed almost any of the many things consultants do.

In either case this section needs to be set out in a way that is 'benefits-led', spelling out the advantages and making clear what the solution will mean to, or do for, the reader as well as specifying the details and/or technical features. Thus do not just list what you will do – describe what the result will be or how a stage will move things forward once completed.

Remember, the total job here is threefold: to explain, to do so persuasively and also to differentiate. Never forget, when putting together a proposal, that you may well be in competition and what you present will be compared, often closely, with the offerings of others. A focus on the needs is usually the best way to ensure the readers' attention; nothing must be said that does not have clear relevance.

One further point is particularly important here: individuality. It is so easy to store standard documents on disk these days, and indeed it may be possible to edit one proposal into a new version that does genuinely suit a similar need elsewhere (though double, double check that you have changed everything necessary, for example, names and any other individual references. I received a proposal once that referred to me as Margaret half way through!) But, if a proposal is intended to look tailored it must be just that and there must be no hint of it seeming standardised. This is sufficiently important to re-emphasise – bespoke proposals must *never* seem standard in any sense. Someone may well know that you write similar documents, but will still appreciate clear signs that you have prepared something 'tailored just for them'.

Only when this section has been covered thoroughly should you move on to refer to costs, because only when it is appreciated exactly what value and benefits are being provided can people consider costs in context.

Costs

Costs must be stated clearly, and not look disguised (though certain techniques for presenting the figures are useful, for example amortising costs – describing something as £1,000 per month, rather than £12,000 for the year; describing and costing stages separately – such as preparing and conducting training). All the necessary detail must be there, including any items that are:

■ options;
■ extras;
■ associated expenses.

These must be shown and made clear. Anything found to cost more than someone first thought tends to be ill-regarded thereafter, and may preclude winning repeat business.

Without going into the details of pricing policy linked to sales proposals, do note that:

- price should be linked as closely as possible to benefits;
- this section must establish or reinforce that you offer value for money, not just state figures baldly;
- invoicing details and trading terms often need including, and must always be clear; mistakes here tend to be expensive (in the United Kingdom remember to make clear whether the price is inclusive of VAT);
- overseas, attention must be given to currency considerations;
- comparisons may need to be made with competition or with past projects;
- range figures (necessary in some kinds of offering) must be used carefully (do not make the gap too wide and never subsequently go over the upper range figure).

Look carefully at how you arrange this section; it is not just facts and numbers, it must be as persuasive as any other part of the document. And note that costs used internally must be as well presented as price is externally to customers.

A question often asked is: won't some people turn straight to the 'costs' section? Yes, without a doubt this happens – indeed, it is only realistic to assume that some (most?) readers will look at this page or pages before reading *anything* else. Certainly for such people there needs to be sufficient explanation given, including cost justification and, above all, clear benefits, linked in here. Just the bald figures can be very off-putting. This section must not only deal with its discrete topic, it must act to persuade the reader who starts by reading the costs section that it is worth turning to the front of the proposal and reading through from the beginning. Write it to achieve just that.

To reinforce points made here about costs, let me quote John de Forte and Guy Jones, who are co-authors of *Proposals, Pitches and Beauty Parades* (Pearson). They focus primarily on the most complex areas of proposing, those where competitive tendering is the best description of what occurs. Here the presentation of price (they focus on fee businesses) is perhaps even more important, but their advice is good for any situation:

> Treat it (presenting the price) as an opportunity to convey positive messages about your commitment to giving value for money and how you intend to help the client monitor and control costs; try to show that you want the service to be as cost-effective as possible... Apart from giving the fee itself, describe also the basis of charging and, if it is a long-term assignment, how fee levels might be determined in the future or when it would be appropriate to review them. If a detailed fee analysis is required, this may be better dealt with in an appendix.

Areas of detail
There are additional topics that it may be necessary to deal with here, as mentioned above: timing, logistics, staffing, etc. Sometimes these are best combined with costs within one section. Not if there are too many perhaps, but, for example, costs and timing go well together, with maybe one other separate, numbered, section dealing with any further topics before moving on.

The principles here are similar to those for handling costs. Matters such as timing must be made completely clear and all possibilities of misunderstanding or omission avoided.

Bear in mind the need for individuality and a tailored approach. For instance, a biographical note about yourself or colleagues needs to be tailored to any specific proposal.

Summary or closing statement
The final section must act to round off the document and it has a number of specific jobs to do. Its first, and perhaps most important, task is of course to summarise. All the threads must be drawn together and key aspects emphasised. A summary fulfils a number of purposes:

▓ It is a useful conclusion for all readers and should ensure the proposal ends on a note that they can easily agree is an effective summary. Because this is often the most difficult part of the document to write, it is also a part that can impress disproportionately. Readers know good summarising is not easy and they respect the writer who achieves it. It is taken as a clear sign of professional competence.

▓ It is useful too in influencing others around the decision maker, who may study the summary but not go through the whole proposal in detail.

▓ It ensures the final word, and the final impression left with the reader, is about benefits and value for money.

In addition, it can be useful to:

▓ recap key points (as well as key benefits);
▓ stress that the proposals are, in effect, the mutual conclusions of both parties (if this is so);
▓ link to action, action dates and details of contact (though this could equally be dealt with in a covering letter);
▓ invoke a sense of urgency (you will normally hope for things to be tied down promptly, but ultimately need to respect the prospect's timing).

There is also what is called an 'Executive Summary', just as with a report. This is a summary placed at the start of a document to do much the same job as one at the end. In part it is a matter of taste (or of what readers want – and you can ask), and sometimes you can utilise both. The only other guide that seems useful is that a traditional summary (at the end) is best for a decision maker. They will read it through and this positioning provides the most logical explanation. For recommenders or others less involved, the executive summary may be preferred. Whichever is used it must be well written, and remember – a short final word remains necessary even when the main summary is placed early on.

Other matters

The key additional thing here is *appendices*. It is important that proposals, like any document, flow. The argument they present must proceed logically and there must be no distractions from the developing picture. Periodically, there is sometimes a need to go into deep detail. Especially if this is technical, tedious or if it involves numerous figures – however necessary the content may be – it is better not to let such detail slow and interrupt the flow of the argument. Such information can usefully be referred to at the appropriate point, but with a note that the 'chapter and verse' of it appears in an appendix. Be specific, saying for example: 'This detail will be found in Appendix 2: *Costs and timing,* which appears on page 21.'

This arrangement can be used for a variety of elements: from terms and conditions of business to details inherent in a project. For example, a proposal about a computer systems project might list recommended hardware details at the end.

A proposal is a detailed document and it is sometimes questioned whether it needs a covering letter. The answer is clear – yes, it does – always. In part it is a courtesy, yet the content of the letter is important, especially so for more complex situations and more elaborate proposals. It will, if it is interesting, be the first thing that is read. It sets the scene for the rest of the message. So it must say more than 'here is the promised proposal' (a compliments slip could do that) and is a useful place to add emphasis, perhaps instilling a sense of urgency, touching on results or setting the scene for any meeting you hope will follow.

Next, assuming proposals arrive safely and are read, there is another possibility that their use may link to – presentations – that needs some thought at the writing stage.

The presentation of proposals

Some proposals are posted just like a letter; once in front of the prospect they must do their work alone, though they may be followed up by letter, e-mail, telephone and so on (persistence here can pay dividends). Incidentally, consider carefully the e-mailing of proposals. This can be satisfactory, especially in sending something to people you know well (or if asked), but it does not put something as smart as a bound document on their desk. Speed may be of the essence sometimes, but you can always follow up an e-mail with a copy sent physically.

Sometimes you know that complex proposals, especially those involving more than one person in the decision, will be the subject of formal presentations. These can happen in two main ways: 1) the proposal is sent, then a presentation is made later to those who have (or should have!) read the document; 2) the presentation is made first, with the detailed proposal being left as a permanent reminder of the presentation's content.

If such an arrangement is made in advance, then the proposal needs to reflect what is to happen. For example, you may need more detail in a proposal that has to stand on its own than one that will follow a presentation. It might sometimes be possible (with agreement) to delay completing the proposal until after a presentation, allowing the inclusion of any final elements stemming from any feedback arising during the presentation meeting. Alternatively you can issue a revised version at this stage, either amending a draft or adding an appendix.

Certainly there should be a close parallel between the two entities so that it is clear how anything being said at a presentation relates to the proposal. Rarely should any of the proposal be read out verbatim. What is usually most important is for additional explanation, examples and exemplification of what has been written to be given verbally.

It may cause confusion if, say, a proposal with eight main headings is discussed at a meeting with nine or ten items being run through (certainly without explanation). It is helpful if you can organise it so that the job of preparing the proposal and the presentation overlap and are kept close.

A final idea here may be useful: more than one company I know prints out – for itself – a 'presentation copy' of the proposal in a larger than normal format or type size. This enables it to be easily referred to by someone standing in presentation style at a meeting. It also gives extra space to annotate the document with any additional notes that will help to guide the presentation along precisely. One caveat here: just remember that page numbers will be different on the different versions and do not let this cause confusion.

Two rules

These are obvious but nevertheless still apt sometimes to be overlooked.

1. Make sure every proposal *looks good*. Use plenty of headings, bold type where appropriate, and make it look professional. Do not cramp it – if it is being passed round the client organisation, room for annotation is useful.
2. Check it carefully – *very, very carefully*. Remember the earlier example of the consulting firm that had a photocopy of the title page of a proposal returned to them. It was sent in an envelope without even a compliments slip. The name of the client's organisation was incorrectly spelt; it was ringed in red and underneath was written 'No thank you!'

The lessons here are vital to a proposal prompting agreement, and many of the points made are applicable more widely than just to proposals. Other major documents stand similar review to ascertain just how their writing should be approached; given the variety of documents used in the workplace comprehensiveness is not possible here.

Brochures and leaflets

Now we spare a few words about other specialist documents, which may be used in a number of ways: for example, brochures distributed by salespeople, leaflets you display in a reception area, or items for staff information, or used from the sales office or for direct mail. There is, however, no reason why such material should be suitable for everything and you may need to produce dedicated material, tailored specifically to one particular task. Here we focus primarily on (corporate) brochures sent by post, whether en mass or one at a time.

In either case, the brochure is unlikely always to set out to tell people 'everything there is to know' about the organisation, product or whatever. Rather it may prompt a desire for discussion. Too much information can even have the effect of reducing responses. One hotel, sending direct mail to promote its conference business, found that the numbers of potential clients coming to inspect the hotel doubled when it replaced a short letter and glossy comprehensive brochure with a longer letter, no brochure and an invitation to visit (because people seeing the full brochure felt no need to visit: they could *see* what the place was like).

The production of brochures generally is an area of increasing professionalism and great care is needed in defining the objective, creating the right message and making sure the brochure looks good and reflects the image that the organisation intends to project. The days of the bland, general brochure, one very similar to those of other industry competitors, which describe the chronological history of the firm and everything it does, and intended to be used for everything, are rapidly passing. What is needed now is the ability to match each objective in every particular area with something specifically designed for the job. This may mean producing separate brochures for each product in a range. It may mean that any 'corporate' brochure is a folder with separate inserts aimed at different target groups or different types of customer. It may mean a revised brochure every year if it is always to be correct and current. It may even mean a difference between the sort of brochure that is right to give a prospective customer after a preliminary meeting and the sort that is suitable to present to an intermediary who may have a role in, say, recommending you to others. It is 'horses for courses', and the specific individual uses and objectives should precede and dictate the writing and the content.

For mailing purposes the brochure or leaflet concerned must be specific to the objective set for the particular promotion. Brochures may need to be reasonably self-standing; after all they may get separated from any covering letter (though the two together almost always produce a better response). However, the total content – letter plus brochure – needs to hang together, to produce a complete and integrated message; this is true of design and message.

Overall, what must be created is something that is accurately directed at a specific group, with a clear objective in mind. This may seem basic; of course, promotional material is there to inform, but it must do so persuasively. That is the prime purpose. But this does not, as comments on persuasiveness made clear, mean moving to something that is inappropriately strident (which might in any case be self-defeating); it does mean putting a clear emphasis on customer need and benefits (what things do for people, rather than what they are).

Essentially, a customer-focused approach (not introspective), and well designed for its purpose, is the rule. What does this mean? It must:

- look good (though good design is much more readily available than good writing);
- be practical (for example for mailing and filing if you hope people will keep it);
- be illustrated in some way (almost always this enhances appearance);
- be readable, interesting and relevant, with its message being put across in a punchy, perhaps novel, way.

There are a few rules to be observed about brochures and those rules that one might define are made to be broken. This is because they must be *creatively* constructed to reflect the image of the firm graphically, differentiate it from its competitors and aim their chosen message directly at the target group addressed. But the copy is perhaps more important than anything. Many brochures have clearly had a good deal of money spent on their design and print, but the text is dull or inappropriate. Start with the copy – taking on board all the principles set out here – and then design the brochure as a vehicle to carry your message.

Making documents look good

Finally, remember that the end product should be neatly presented. This principle applies to every kind of document, but perhaps especially to longer ones, so a word about it is added here. Basics first: any message must look right. It must be attractively laid out, grammatically correct and well presented. This is especially important if the message is difficult (controversial, needing to persuade, etc) since it gives the impression that it has originated from a professional source.

For letters, the letterhead itself is important to the image: an up to date yet not 'over the top' design is what should be aimed at and this is not easy. Subjective judgements are involved. Ultimately, it is a matter of opinion and in smaller organisations this can sometimes mean a safe compromise that may dilute impact. Consider, too, whether your standard letterhead is right for every purpose. For instance, direct mail purposes may demand something different: one with all the contact information at the foot of the page, allowing a heading and perhaps more to go at the top.

To ensure the finishing touches and add impact you should think about the following.

- Position letters on the page according to the amount of the text. It is unattractive if there is a huge expanse of white below a very short letter. Position it lower down, in that case, or consider having two sizes of letterhead paper printed and put short letters on the smaller sheets.
- 'Block' paragraphs, with double spacing between each paragraph for greater clarity and smartness.
- Leave at least 1½ inches at the foot of the page before going onto the second page; leave a bigger space to avoid having only one or two lines (plus farewells) on the second page. A good deal of business material ends up annotated in some way, and more space makes this easier for people to do.
- Allow enough space on a letter for the signature, name and job title. It is better to carry the letter over on to another page, than cram it in at the bottom.

- Note, at the foot of the last page, all the enclosures mentioned in the text and sent with the letter.
- Staple the pages together to avoid losses.
- Always number pages.
- Number the paragraphs when a lot of points have to be covered.
- <u>Underline</u> all headings or make them **bold**.

Remember: layout must reflect the style, the reader and the emphasis of the points being made. For example, it can bolster a persuasive message by helping create emphasis and put over a feeling of efficiency (in the way, for instance, that listing enclosures can do).

Graphic emphasis can help keep people reading, guide them through longer texts and simply create a feeling of accessibility and care that itself promotes readability. Such emphasis can be made, in this age of word-processing, in a number of ways, with:

CAPITALS
<u>Underlining</u>
   Indenting
Bold type
Italics
~~COLOUR~~

While these features should not be overdone, they can be useful and, in whatever form and combination you select, should be well placed. As an example consider this book and others like it. It has (if the typesetter has done their job well) a modern look. Space is as important as what is there, and the overall effect is designed to make the text seem accessible, both as you flick through on first picking up the book and on reading it. It is very different to the 'textbook style' of old. The overall layout, especially the number of headings, is important to its looking accessible and readable.

Anything that looks a mess is likely to be taken as a mess: ill thought out and giving its reader little confidence in what is to come if they read it. The reverse is true too: a well-presented document will always enhance its content, particularly early on when potential readers are still deciding how much attention to give it and how seriously to take it.

Writing tight

The phrase on page 102 that I suggested you attempted to abbreviate is 27 words long. The following, encapsulating much the same message, consists of only 10 words:

> Although he succeeded, he soon regretted using so many words.

I used this as an exercise on a training course not so long ago and one inventive participant reduced it further – to three words: 'Successful, but verbose' (and it very nearly does capture the full message of the 27-word original version!). Certainly this is a good skill to develop. The phrase above is not, of course, set out as the only right one; there are many alternatives and as always circumstances will dictate what's best.

Reducing, again by more than half, the second two phrases, you might get:

> Rising property values will make home-buying more difficult. *(9 words)*

> John ignored the results because he distrusted the analytical techniques. *(10 words)*

You might look too at other things you have written recently and see if they contain sentences or paragraphs that are too long, that can easily be abbreviated and made to read better while conveying the same meaning. Try it.

Postscript

> I am a bear of very little brain, and long words
> bother me.
>
> *A A Milne,* Winnie the Pooh

Finally, let us use a little exercise to make one last point, and perhaps prompt you to action. Take a moment to read the following paragraph and see if you can answer the question it poses:

> As you scan this short paragraph, try to spot what is unusual about it. Half an hour is normal for many to find a solution that is both logical and satisfactory to its originator. I do not say that anything is 'wrong' about it, simply that it is unusual. You may want to study its grammatical construction to find a solution, but that is not a basis of its abnormality, nor is its lack of any information, logical points or conclusion. If you work in communications you may find that an aid to solving this particular conundrum. It is not about anagrams, synonyms, antonyms or acrostics, but it is unusual. So, why is that?

The answer is shown on page 128. This is only a bit of fun, but it makes an important point: to write well you must read (though not *War and Peace* unless you want to!). The more interest you take in language, then the more it will influence you. There is no harm in copying examples of style and approach that appeal to you, nor is there in adapting and tweaking things for your own purpose. For instance, I noticed only recently the device of the sentence turned into one-word sentences to create emphasis. It. Really. Works. And, like much else, provided it is not overused, it adds to the power to make the point you want. As well as reading, and observing more consciously, books or indeed anything else, keep an eye out for things that might particularly help. For example, if you have to write sales letters, keep a file of those that come to you (you might file them in two categories: those with good things in them and those that demonstrate what to avoid!).

Last, a recommendation: always have by you a good dictionary, a thesaurus (something for which curiously there appears to be only one word! And which is a dictionary of synonyms) and a good guide to grammar. Something like the *Good Word Guide* (Bloomsbury) is useful, but I would also recommend a book by the novelist and columnist Keith Waterhouse, *English our English* (Penguin). This is the only grammar book you might actually enjoy reading. It is full of good advice, of enthusiasm for language and in places it is amusing. It will tell you when to use a colon rather than a semi-colon, but it will also encourage you to break a few rules and make your writing more interesting. I have read and reread it; and could usefully do so again.

Ultimately what constitutes the best business writing is not something that follows a slavish set of rules; rather it is what works. So do note, and record, your successes and failures and use what you have done to assist you in future. Some ideas or approaches may become part of your style. Others may be used again and doing so even once may be useful. Similarly, analysis will have you resolving never to do some things again. Experimentation is a useful part of the process, but so is learning from experience.

Written communication presents one of the greatest, and perhaps also easiest, opportunities to shine as a communicator. Because prevailing standards are not so good, many people find writing a chore and respect anyone who can do it well. So let me end by emphasising four points. Whatever the nature of the documents you must create, always:

1. Prepare thoroughly, and set clear objectives, before you 'put pen to paper' as it were.
2. Bear all your intentions in mind throughout the process.
3. Write throughout with a focus on the reader.
4. Use language, consciously, to make what you say powerful, descriptive, memorable and more.

Some of the ideas presented in the previous pages may well help you, but remember what the US essayist Clarence Day said: 'Information's pretty thin stuff, unless mixed with experience. At the end of the day what will make your written messages work – is you.'

Finally, as a final reminder of some of the things that make for good writing, this checklist (reproduced unashamedly from my book *How to Write Reports and Proposals*) makes some good points in a light-hearted way.

Some memorably put writing rules

- Don't abbrev things inappropriately.
- Check to see if you any words out.
- Be careful to use adjectives and adverbs correct.
- About sentences fragments.
- Don't use no double negatives.
- Just between you and I, case is important.
- Join clauses good, like a conjunction should.
- Don't use commas, that aren't necessary.
- Its important to use apostrophe's right.
- It's better not to unnecessarily split infinitives.
- Only Proper Nouns should be capitalised. also a sentence should begin with a capital and end with a full stop
- Use hyphens in compound-words, not just in any two-word phrase.

- In letters reports and things like that we use commas to keep a string of items apart.
- Watch out for irregular verbs that have creeped into your language.
- Verbs has to agree with their subjects.
- A writer mustn't change your point of view.
- A preposition isn't a good thing to end a sentence with.
- Avoid clichés like the plague.

Answer to the exercise on page 125

The answer is that, unusually, the paragraph contains no letter 'e'. This is the most commonly appearing letter in the English language; normally writing any amount of text without one would be quite difficult, and certainly is rarely seen.

The author

For a book like this the author's pedigree, as it were, especially in terms of writing is perhaps important. Patrick Forsyth runs Touchstone Training & Consultancy, specialising in the improvement of marketing, management and communications skills.

He is the author of more than 50 successful business books including the following, which are also published by Kogan Page:

Marketing and Selling Professional Services
Marketing Stripped Bare
Getting a Top Job in Marketing
Getting a Top Job in Sales and Business Development

And also in the Creating Success series:

Successful Time Management
How to Motivate People
How to Write Reports and Proposals

Improve your Coaching and Training Skills
Developing your Staff

Past reviews have said of his writing, 'Refreshingly useful and easy to read', and 'Packed with solid advice'. Numerous translations of many of his titles have appeared around the world; to date in 23 languages.

He has also written many articles for journals such as *Better Business* and *Professional Marketing*. He has acted as editorial advisor to publishers, co-written books (one with a co-author in Australia), ghost-written books, written and produced corporate publications and undertaken copy writing work, and reviewed books for Amazon, The Good Book Guide and newBooks. He has also written more general material too, including a humorous look at office life in *Surviving Office Politics*, and a couple of light-hearted travel books. One, about a journey on the Eastern & Oriental Express, is titled *First Class at Last!*; a second, *A Land Like None You Know*, is to be published soon.

To respond to anything written in this book, please contact the author on patrick@touchstonetc.freeserve.co.uk.

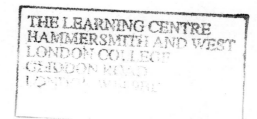

THE LEARNING CENTRE
HAMMERSMITH AND WEST
LONDON COLLEGE
GLIDDON ROAD
LONDON W14 9BL

The sharpest minds
need the finest advice

visit
www.koganpage.com
today

You're reading one of the thousands of books published by Kogan Page, Europe's largest independent business publisher. We publish a range of books and electronic products covering business, management, marketing, logistics, HR, careers and education. Visit our website today and sharpen your mind with some of the world's finest thinking.

KOGAN
PAGE